STUDIES IN THE UK ECONOMY

The European Community

Brian Hill

University of Nottingham

GW00726166

Series Editor
Bryan Hurl
Head of Economics, Harrow School

HEINEMANN
EDUCATIONAL

Heinemann Educational,
a division of Heinemann Educational Books Ltd,
Halley Court, Jordan Hill, Oxford OX2 8EJ

OXFORD LONDON EDINBURGH
MADRID ATHENS BOLOGNA PARIS
MELBOURNE SYDNEY AUCKLAND SINGAPORE TOKYO
IBADAN NAIROBI HARARE GABORONE
PORTSMOUTH NH (USA)

First published 1991

British Library Cataloguing in Publication Data
Hill, Brian
The European Community. – (Studies in the UK economy)
1. European Community. Economic conditions
I. Title II. Series
330.94

ISBN 0-435-33010-1

Typeset and illustrated by Gecko Limited, Bicester, Oxon
Printed and bound by Clays Ltd, St Ives plc

Acknowledgements
The Publishers would like to thank the following for permission to
reproduce copyright material:
Anti-Common Market League for the cartoons on pp. 20, 75; Associated
Newspapers Ltd for the cartoons on pp. 4, 5; Associated Examining Board
for the questions on pp. 51, 60, 71; BBC Enterprises for the extract on
p. 26 from YES, PRIME MINISTER by Jonathan Lynn and Anthony Jay;
EC Commision for the extract on p. 74; *The Economist* for the articles on
pp. 10 – 11, 16 – 17, 32 – 33, 84 and the charts on p.84; Epson Ltd for the
advertisement on pp. 37 – 39; *The Financial Times* for the table on p. 67;
Reproduced with the permission of Her Majesty's Stationery Office: the
extract on p.57, the statistics on pp. 78, 80 from the Central Statisical
Office; Joint Matriculation Board for the questions on p. 36; Office for
Official Publications of the European Community for the extracts and
statistics on pp. 2, 13, 22, 27, 34, 47, 66, 68, 69, 76, 77, 85, 86; Oxford
and Cambridge Schools Examination Board for the questions on pp. 37, 51,
60, 71; Times Newspapers Ltd for the articles on pp. 30 – 31, 44, 44 – 45,
52; University of Cambridge Local Examinations Syndicate for the
questions on p. 23; University of London School Examinations Board for
the questions on pp. 36 - 37, 51, 83; University of Oxford Delegacy of
Local Examinations for the questions on pp. 23, 51; Welsh Joint Education
Committee for the questions on pp. 52, 82. Thanks are also due to Charles
Smith for the Data Response Questions on pp. 23 – 24, 71 – 72.

The Publishers have made every effort to contact the correct copyright
holders. However, if any material has been incorrectly acknowledged, the
Publishers would be happy to make the necessary arrangements at the
earliest opportunity.

Contents

Preface

Now that the UK has joined the Exchange Rate Mechanism, the importance to our lives of membership of the EC is becoming recognized on a greater scale. Indeed, to pretend otherwise is to ignore economic realities and our obligations to the Treaty of Rome.

Over half of the UK's trade is with the Community, and this figure will continue to rise. The 1990s will see the burgeoning of EC competition policy, regional policy and, after 1992, a true 'common market'. Planned Economic and Monetary Union will split the electorate over the vexed question of sovereignty. Students must place the UK economy within the context of the wider EC framework.

The agreement of eleven of the twelve EC members to proceed to stages two and three of the Delors plan left the UK apart – with, at one stage, a prime minister who described the proposals as 'living in cloud cuckoo land'. As the rhetoric gathers momentum, informed debate is swamped by populist sentiment. Brian Hill demonstrates his experience as a teacher with a disinterested text, lightly written, but offering clarity to the student of the EC.

Bryan Hurl
Series Editor

Chapter One

Origins of the European Community

The Common Market began in 1958 but the UK did not join until 1973 –and still has mixed feelings about membership.

What is the European Community, often referred to as 'the Common Market'? It is a combination of twelve West European countries which have decided that their future wellbeing will be enhanced by their union. They are gradually evolving from independent sovereign states to a federation or 'United States of Europe'. This process of integration is both economic and political. Whilst this book concentrates upon the economic aspects it must not be forgotten that the fundamental forces involved are political, and so, not surprisingly, are controversial.

In this chapter the forces which have led to the creation of the Community are briefly outlined and its objectives are analysed against this background. Finally, the Community institutions and the way in which decisions are taken and implemented are examined.

Table 1 gives some basic data on the size and composition of the Community, and comparative data for the United States of America and Japan. As the latter two countries are the Community's major competitors they will be included in many tables throughout the book.

Historical background

At the conclusion of the Second World War, Europe was devastated. It was also fundamentally politically divided into a communist East and a capitalist West. The West included Germany and Italy who, with Japan, had fought on one side in the war, whilst the opposing side, the Allies, had included much of the rest of continental Europe in addition to Russia, the USA and the British Empire. Soviet Russia and the USA were much larger and more powerful than any other country. Some West European countries feared that their weakened condition constituted a power vacuum which might be too tempting for their huge eastern neighbour. They came together in defence

Table 1 The European Community in perspective, 1987

	Area (1000 km²)	Population (millions)	GDP (milliard ECU)
Belgium	31	9.9	120
Denmark	43	5.1	88
West Germany	249	61.1	970
Greece	132	10.0	41
Spain	505	38.7	251
France	544	55.4	764
Ireland	69	3.5	25
Italy	301	57.2	659
Luxembourg	3	0.4	5
Netherlands	41	14.6	185
Portugal	92	10.2	32
United Kingdom	244	56.8	580
EC (12)	2253	322.8	3721
USA	9373	241.6	3904
Japan	372	121.5	2061

Source: *Basic Statistics of the Community*, 26th edn., 1989

treaties and to cooperate in economic reconstruction.

In the immediate post-war years many economists and politicians produced plans for a better and more secure future. One of the most influential was the French economist **Jean Monnet**. He envisaged a united Europe in which union would bring peace and prosperity to an area where nationalistic division and rivalry had imposed a tradition of war and misery. He was convinced that a worthwhile future for Europe required economic and political union. The latter had to be a long-term aim since it was unthinkable in the immediate aftermath of bloodshed and bitterness. So he conceived union by degrees, moving gradually from economic cooperation to **economic integration**, ultimately with full **political union** as the desired end.

Monnet's vision was given practical expression through the efforts of skilled politicians such as Dr Conrad Adenauer of Germany, Robert Schuman of France and Paul-Henri Spaak of Belgium. What role did the UK play? None. The UK emerged from the war as the only major West European country not to be conquered. She was greatly weakened but was still a world power and still possessed an enormous Empire. The latter absorbed British political attention, particularly as the Empire was being turned into a Commonwealth as its members were given sovereignty over their own destinies. So the UK lost the opportunity of playing a leading role in shaping the new Europe.

After the war the Allies retained control of Germany's coal and steel, regarded as the basic materials of war, via the International Ruhr Authority. Handing back control of these raw materials was regarded as dangerous, yet they were essential to German economic recovery. A plan to resolve this problem was put forward in 1950. It proposed the formation of a common market in these materials, thus giving Germany access to them but making it impossible for any one nation to gain control, which instead would be in the hands of a supranational authority. The UK was invited to join this organization but declined – Prime Minister Atlee said in the Commons that his party was '. . . not prepared to accept the principle that the most vital economic forces of this country should be handed over to an authority that is utterly undemocratic . . .'. This dismissive attitude to European integration was typical of both politicians and public in the UK at that time. Nevertheless the **European Coal and Steel Community (ECSC)** was created by the **Treaty of Paris** in 1951, the signatories being France, West Germany, Italy, the Netherlands, Belgium and Luxembourg. These countries (**the Six**) discussed further integration intermittently during the next few years but each time negotiations failed. Eventually in 1955, Benelux (a customs union formed by Belgium, the Netherlands and Luxembourg in 1948) proposed the formation of a common market, arguing that political union, although the desired long-term aim, could not be achieved without prior economic integration. The Six received this idea favourably and formed a committee presided over by Paul-Henri Spaak, to prepare the ground for a treaty. The UK was invited to join this committee but again declined. Following prolonged and detailed negotiations the **Treaty of Rome** was formulated; it was signed on 25 March 1957, creating the **European Economic Community** (EEC) from 1 January 1958.

The Six also founded a European Atomic Energy Community (Euratom) with an additional Rome treaty signed in 1957. Initially the three Communities remained separate, but in 1965 under the **Treaty of Brussels** their executives were merged from 1967 (although the three treaties have never been consolidated into a new merged treaty) and the term 'European Community' is now taken to include all three Communities, although colloquially and in this book it usually refers principally to the economic component.

Enlargement of the Community

Although the UK did not relish economic integration and the implied loss of sovereignty which this entailed, it did see much sense in cooperation in terms of free trade. Along with other countries having similar attitudes – the traditionally neutral countries – the UK tried to avoid the economic isolation which being outside the EC implied, by forming a free trade area. The **European Free Trade Area** (EFTA) came into being under the **Stockholm Convention**, signed on 4 January 1960. Its signatories were the UK, Austria, Denmark, Norway, Portugal, Sweden and Switzerland; EFTA was confined to trade in manufactures.

By the early 1960s the British government had changed its attitude to the Community. The UK's relative decline as a world power and changing trading patterns convinced British politicians that membership of the Community was desirable. In 1961 Harold Macmillan, the Conservative Prime Minister, announced that the UK would apply to join. This was not a popular move, sentiment being fairly conveyed by the two *Daily Mail* cartoons reproduced here. Complicated negotiations followed, but they failed after two years when the French President, General de Gaulle, expressed the opinion that Britain was not yet sufficiently European to be admitted. In a change of government, Labour came to power and in 1967 Prime Minister Harold Wilson announced a new membership application. By the end of the year General de Gaulle had again effectively vetoed UK membership by announcing that such an event would

Brig.-Gen. GULLY SQUARE-LEGG, M.C.C.
(President Empire Umpires' Club)

"They'll be wanting us to play French cricket next, dammit!"

destroy the Community. However, in 1969 he resigned and the Six agreed to open negotiations with the UK, Denmark, Ireland and Norway. The first three subsequently became full members on 1 January 1973. Although Norwegian negotiations also succeeded, the Norwegian people rejected membership in a referendum.

Fred Uppe

(Secretary, Fish Porter's Union)

*'I don't want ter be a member of no ******** Common Market, mate!'*

Further enlargements of the Community added Greece in 1981 and Portugal and Spain in 1986. All three countries had emerged from dictatorships immediately before making their applications to join, and saw the Community as offering political stability as well as economic benefits. These various enlargements of the Community are a source of confusion to the unwary: obviously EC data refer to a different mix of countries over time. A useful, but unfortunately not universal, convention is to write EC(6), EC(9), EC(10) and EC(12) to indicate which version of the Community is being discussed. In this book most data relate to EC(12) even for years before 1986 – by the simple expedient of adding figures for the non-members to the EC data.

Objectives of the European Economic Community

These are best expressed by quoting in full Article 2 of the Treaty of Rome:

> *It shall be the aim of the Community, by establishing a Common Market and progressively approximating the economic policies of Member States, to promote throughout the Community a harmonious development of economic activities, a continuous and balanced expansion, an increased stability, an accelerated raising of the standard of living and closer relations between its Member States.*

This article makes it clear that a common market is expected to be of economic benefit to its members. It ends by looking towards 'closer relations between its Member States', implying that economic progress will lead towards some degree of political integration. This is consistent with the vision of Monnet mentioned earlier.

Although the prime aims of the Community are naturally directed towards its own members, its founding fathers were not entirely inward-looking. Article 110 says that the Community intends to contribute '. . . to the harmonious development of world trade, the progressive abolition of restrictions on international exchanges and the lowering of customs barriers'. Article 237 says that 'Any European State may apply to become a member of the Community . . .'.

What is a common market?

The economic principles are to be discussed in the next chapter. For the moment a brief answer is that it is a group of countries which have no trade barriers between its members, but with a common agreed trade policy towards third countries. Goods, services, labour and capital can circulate freely within and between members as the forces of free competition dictate. Since one of the main functions of government is to intervene in the national economy, some coordination of such interventions is essential to prevent the distortion of competitive forces by different government policies operating in the member states. Clearly this coordination requires organizing and the Community has special Community level institutions to do this.

Community institutions

There are four major bodies: the **European Commission, the Council of Ministers, the European Parliament and the Court of Justice.**

The Commission is the civil service of the Community. It develops policies in the sense of drafting proposals, discussing them with the Council of Ministers, Parliament and a variety of interested parties. When policies have been decided it sees to their implementation as **Directives, Decisions** and **Regulations.** All three types of outcome have the force of law throughout member states – *if they conflict with national legislation it is the Community law which must prevail.* Directives take effect through national legislatures, which are required to produce their own laws along the prescribed policy lines; that is, laws to implement decisions are tailored to suit different national circumstances. A Decision is binding upon a named person, company or state. Regulations are more general, applying in an identical fashion throughout the Community.

When a policy has been agreed by the Council of Ministers, the Commission organizes its execution, often with the aid of national civil services. Indeed most of the day-to-day implementation of policies is in the hands of national civil servants acting virtually as agents of the Community. The Commission is too small to do anything more than supervise in this field – far from being the vast 'Brussels bureaucracy' imagined by some nationalists it employs less than half the number of civil servants one would find in some of the larger UK ministries.

The Commission has 17 members appointed by member states, each representing a major policy area. The professional civil servants working under them are divided into 22 **Directorates-General** (DGs). These are similar to ministries in the UK. Some of the big ones of immediate interest to economists are DG IV – Competition, DG VI - Agriculture, and DG VII – Transport.

The Council of Ministers is not a fixed body of individuals: its composition depends on the policy in question. For example, if the topic is agriculture it is comprised of the Ministers of Agriculture from each member state, for transport policy the Ministers of Transport form the Council. All decisions are taken by the Council of Ministers. They receive proposals from the Commission, they may instruct the Commission to formulate a particular policy, they adopt and amend policies. As the Council is formed of national politicians it is to be expected that much political 'horse trading' takes place which may result in agreements involving unrelated issues despite the best efforts of the Commission.

The European Council is a special council of *heads of state or government* which meets twice a year. This council takes the major decisions of principle which determine the nature and direction of Community activities.

The European Parliament is a directly elected body of 518 members sitting in Strasbourg. It is largely a consultative body, receiving and commenting on Commission proposals before they are adopted by the Council. The latter can pass laws even if the Parliament disagrees with them. However, the Parliament does have some budgetary power and in particular can reject the Community draft budget, which it did in 1985, forcing a new budget to be formulated. It can also, by a two-thirds majority, dismiss the Commission, though it would have no say in the appointment of replacements.

The Court of Justice is based in Luxembourg. It has 13 judges, including one from each member state. The Court's judgements are binding throughout the Community. Indeed member states or institutions can be taken to the Court by individuals, organizations, other institutions or other member states.

There are numerous other cogs in the Community machine. Many represent the interests of various branches of manufacture and commerce, workers and consumers. All are provided with opportunities to express their opinions on proposed developments. Only two will be mentioned here, the Committee of Permanent Representatives (COREPER), and the Economic and Social Committee (ECOSOC). The former's 'permanent representatives' are the heads of national delegations to the Community and provide a link between the Commission and national governments. ECOSOC is an advisory body with members drawn from all walks of life; it scrutinizes all Commission proposals.

Decision-making and the Single European Act

The Treaty of Rome allowed for decisions to be reached by unanimous agreement during the early years of the Community. Later, with growing political and economic cohesion, decisions were to be reached through a system of qualified majority voting. In practice, member states were very reluctant to give up the power of veto which the unanimity rule implied. Getting the agreement of all member states was never easy and proved increasingly difficult as the Community was enlarged, so that policy initiatives necessary for the development of the Community were only reached after protracted negotiations. By the early 1980s the Community seemed to be grinding to a halt.

Following much discussion in European Councils and the reports of special committees it was agreed to 'relaunch' the Community via a **Single European Act** (SEA) which was signed by all member states in February 1986. This Act is of great economic and political significance. Its economic impact is to produce a single European market by the abolition of internal barriers to trade by the end of 1992. To this end decisions in the commercial field are now to be reached by qualified majority voting.

Figure 1 outlines the Community legislation process which now operates. This part of the Act and its consequences will be referred to frequently throughout the rest of this book. The qualified majority voting system gives ten votes each to France, Italy, West Germany and the UK, eight to Spain, five each to Belgium, Greece, the

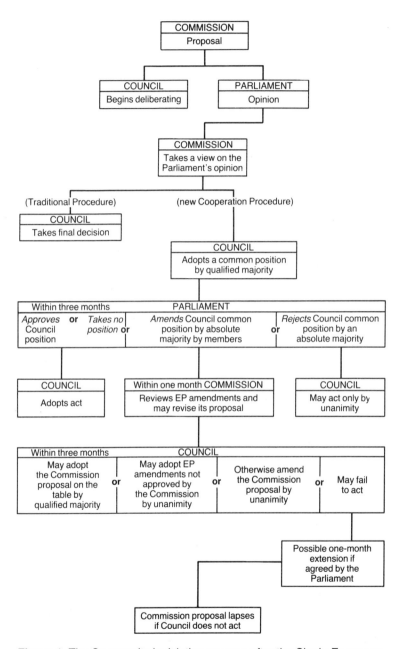

Figure 1 The Community legislative process after the Single European Act (based on a diagram in *The Single European Market*, HMSO)

Netherlands and Portugal, three each to Denmark and Ireland and two to Luxembourg. The total is 76, and 54 represents a qualified majority. The six largest votes add up to 53, so they cannot impose their views on the smaller countries.

The political dimension of the Act is the agreement for further political cooperation. For example, the member states are to work together to formulate a European Foreign Policy, which is indeed a major commitment, a milestone on the road towards political union – though progress towards the next milestone seems slow.

UK membership

The article 'Excuse me, is this the right bus?', reproduced from *The Economist* of 17 December 1988, admirably summarizes the UK's ambivalent position. This book will attempt to provide the facts necessary for an answer, but leaves readers to form their own conclusions.

Excuse me, is this the right bus?

The British pride themselves on their history. But they cite it selectively. In her now famous speech in Bruges last September, Mrs Margaret Thatcher said Britain's European commitment had a long history, dating back to the Roman empire and early Christendom. She dwelt on Britain's past contribution to Europe's freedom through two world wars, and today through the 70,000 British troops permanently stationed on the continent. She rightly stressed that Europe was bigger than the EEC: Prague and Warsaw are great European cities as

much as Paris and Brussels.

Mrs Thatcher said nothing about the two European buses Britain has recently missed: when the Schuman plan for a coal and steel community was proposed in 1950, and when the 1955 Messina conference led to the formation of the EEC itself. Britain eventually heaved itself on board the bus in 1973. Today's fear is that it might fluff the 1992 connection.

The 1950s bus-missings were all the odder because it was Churchill who called in 1947 for a "united states of Europe". His idea was that Britain, with its empire and its special relationship with America, would lead the rest. By the 1950s the empire was disappearing, though Britain's pretensions to great-power status lingered on. It was a time of rebel-fighting in Cyprus and Malaya, of invasion at Suez. Britain had been a founder-member of NATO. Politicians reckoned they could ignore the cranking up of the EEC bus.

Subsequent attempts to hop aboard were rebuffed by de Gaulle, reluctant to give up French leadership of his idea of Europe. By the time Mr Edward Heath took Britain "into Europe", the EEC's long economic boom was petering out. The next 15 years, under Labour and Tory governments alike, were spent in squabbling: over Britain's entrance fee, and over the extravagance of the Community's farm policy. The squabbles are (for the moment) over, but they have left many Britons deeply suspicious of Brussels. British suspicions surface readily, thanks to Europe's slickest machine for co-ordinating EEC policy. Where a Spaniard or Dutchman might wait to see what others think of a Europroposal before reacting – or hope that others will take the blame for blocking it – their British counterpart will trumpet a carefully thought-out, inflexible and often hostile view straight away.

The Community Budget

The Community Budget is very different from national budgets in that its only purpose is to finance common policies and administration. So it does not involve taxation, borrowing, deficits, the redistribution of monies or any of the other functions of a national budget.

The current budget framework was agreed in 1970 and fully operational by 1975. It then had three sources of income – import duties, agricultural import levies and a VAT element. Under the system of common tariffs, import duties and levies are collected at the point of entry regardless of the destination of the imports once within the Community. Thus imports to Germany which arrive at Rotterdam are subject to duty there; clearly it is more reasonable to pay such duties into a common budget than for them to accrue to the member country of the port of origin. Ten per cent of the duties and levies are assumed to be collection costs and are retained by the country of the port of origin.

Two important points must be made regarding the VAT element. First, the VAT is not a Community tax, it only provides a basis for calculating member state contributions to the budget. The Commission calculates the yield which a VAT on a uniform basis would provide if levied in each member country. So this element of the budget relates to a notional VAT. Secondly, the VAT contributions are a balancing item in the budget. The budget is required to balance, and so the VAT element is variable to make this possible. In 1970 the maximum rate of VAT was set at 1 per cent. The structure of the budget is shown in Table 2.

Table 2 Structure of the EC Budget 1975–85

Expenditure	Revenue
Common policies	Import duties
Administration	Agricultural levies
	Up to 1% VAT (balancing item)

Budget problems

There have been two very persistent difficulties. First, budget expenditures began to exceed revenues by 1984 owing to excessive spending on agriculture, which will be discussed in Chapter 4. Second, the Budget treated the UK unfairly, leading to many disagreements and soured relationships; this will be discussed in Chapter 7. Here, the focus of attention is on the fact that expenditure tended to exceed revenue.

The Commission and the Council of Ministers draft the budget for the following financial year (which is also the calendar year) and present it to Parliament. Although the European Parliament can criticize the draft and suggest amendments, its real power is to refuse to adopt the budget, for which it needs a two-thirds majority of votes cast, which must also be a majority of members. In 1979 the EP disapproved of the draft budget for 1980 on the grounds that it gave too much to agriculture and left too little for other policies. In December it threw out the budget by 288 votes to 64, so the Community entered the new year with no budget. How can the Community operate without a budget? The rules permit it to spend on a *'twelfths' basis* – that is, in each month it can spend one-twelfth of the previous year's expenditure; income continues to flow into the budget from import duties and levies. A new budget was not agreed until July 1980, almost overlapping with the draft budget for the following year. The twelfths system also came into operation for part of 1985 and briefly in 1987 following the rejection of draft budgets.

In 1984 spending on agriculture was increased so much that it became clear that the budget needed either to breach the VAT ceiling or to suspend payments. In the event it was saved by delaying some payments until the following year and by 'repayable advances' made by member states. The 1984 crisis concentrated minds sufficiently for the Council of Ministers to agree measures to curb agricultural spending, and this was followed by agreement in the European Council meeting at Fontainebleau to raise the VAT ceiling to 1.4 per cent from 1986 and adopt a solution to the UK budgetary problem. However, the draft budget for 1985 lacked the extra resources to be made available for 1986 and was rejected by the Parliament. Eventually the 1985 budget was agreed and balanced by additional member contributions.

The budget was close to exhaustion in 1986 and 1987. In June 1988 it was agreed to add a fourth source of income (to act retrospectively from 1 January 1988). This is a GNP-based contribution from members, with the total budgetary expenditure limited to 1.15, 1.17, 1.18, 1.19 and 1.2 per cent of the EC's GNP in the years 1988 to 1992 respectively. Both this budget agreement and the 1984 Fontainebleau settlement involved curbs on agricultural spending, though their effectiveness has not been very impressive. Table 3 illustrates the revised structure of the budget with data for 1988; it shows the dominant position of agricultural spending and that total spending is close to the permitted limit.

Table 3 The Community Budget, 1988

Expenditure		Revenue(million ECU)	
Agricultural support	30 893	Agricultural & sugar levies	2 609
Regional Fund	2 980	Customs duties	9 309
Social Fund	2 600	VAT own resource	23 927
Fisheries	281	GNP-based own resource†	6 075
Administration	1 271	Other*	1 501
Repayments to member states	2 534		
Other	3 261		
Total	43 820	Total	43 421

* Other revenues are mainly budget and VAT balancing items from previous years; similar additions will appear in future budgets to balance this one. † Maximum permitted level 1.15% of GNP, 1.09% used.

Source: *XXII General Report on the Activities of the Community*, 1988

```
┌─────────────────────────────────────────────────────────────┐
│                         KEY WORDS                           │
│                                                             │
│  Jean Monnet                  Stockholm Convention          │
│  Economic integration         European Commission          │
│  Political union              Council of Ministers          │
│  European Coal and Steel      European Parliament           │
│    Community                  Court of Justice              │
│  Treaty of Paris              Directives                    │
│  The Six                      Decisions                     │
│  Treaty of Rome               Regulations                   │
│  European Economic            Directorates-General          │
│    Community                  Single European Act           │
│  Treaty of Brussels           The Community Budget          │
│  European Free Trade Area                                   │
└─────────────────────────────────────────────────────────────┘
```

Reading list

Swann, D., *The Economics of the Common Market*, 6th edn, Penguin Books, 1988.

Essay topics

1. Discuss the reasons for the formation of the Common Market. Did the three newest members join for these same reasons?
2. Explain how Community decisions are reached and consider if these procedures can fairly be described as democratic?
3. Why did the UK decide not to join the European Community initially, but then joined later?

Chapter Two

Common Market economics

Economics is often said (by non-economists) to be irrelevant to real life. Wags have observed that 'if all the economists in the world were laid end to end they wouldn't reach a conclusion'. Nevertheless standard economic theory underlies the organization of the European Community in general and its '1992 programme' in particular.

This chapter attempts to answer the question – what are the economic benefits of a common market? On the theoretical side the gains from trade are analysed and related to different levels of economic integration. Finally, the expected size of gains to be achieved by the EC are discussed. This sets the scene for the remaining chapters which examine the operations of the EC in attempting to achieve these theoretical gains.

The gains from trade

Fundamental to any study of trade is the **Law of Comparative Advantage.** Most readers will be familiar with this law, but a thorough understanding should be ensured by studying the accompanying explanation from *The Economist* of 22 September 1990. Briefly, the law states that even if one country is absolutely more efficient in the production of every good than is some second country, if each country specializes in the production of the products in which it has a comparative advantage (i.e. greatest relative efficiency – it produces the goods it is best at producing), then trade will benefit both countries.

The benefits of trade due to comparative advantage are reinforced by **economies of size** (usually referred to incorrectly as economies of scale – see Eckert and Leftwich). This refers to the fact that, for many forms of production, average costs decline as output is expanded, at least until very large outputs are achieved (see any textbook of economic theory). Specialization according to comparative advantage means that firms will have larger markets and will be enabled to grow larger, and hence have lower costs. This is a **dynamic process,** for large firms with low costs and high profits are able to

How to make comparative advantage work for you

These days politicians all over the world declare themselves in favour of *free trade*. When it comes to voting for it, they are not so sure. The reason is not just the pressure of special-interest politics. It is also that most people have imbibed the prejudice that free trade is a good thing, without imbibing the economics that ought to lie behind it. What this prejudice says, in fact, is that free trade is a good thing only if everybody else joins in; one-sided, or unilateral, free trade is a mug's game. The classical case for free trade argues exactly the opposite: free trade is good for a country even if other countries do not return the favour.

Writing 40 years before Ricardo, Adam Smith had already had a lot to say about the gains from trade. He saw it as, among other things, a way of promoting efficiency, both because it fostered competition and because it provided opportunities to specialise and gain economies of scale. Specialisation was a matter of absolute advantage: trade allows countries to produce what they are best at, and buy in the rest.

This view begged a question: what if Britain, say, is bad at making everything? Does this not mean that trade would drive all its producers out of business? David Ricardo answered the question by formulating the principle of comparative advantage. This is perhaps the single most powerful idea in economics.

Help yourself to wine and cheese
Suppose there are two countries, Utopia and Flatland, and that these countries use labour to produce just two goods, wine and cheese. In Utopia it takes one hour of labour to make a pound of cheese and two hours of labour to make a gallon of wine. In Flatland it takes six hours to make a pound of cheese and three hours to make a gallon of wine. Note that Utopia is more productive than Flatland in both goods; it has an absolute advantage in wine and cheese. But its greater advantage, its comparative advantage, is in cheese. This will determine what happens when the two countries trade.

The precise outcome will depend on the pattern of demand, and hence on the price of each good in terms of the other once trade begins. Assume that a pound of cheese trades for a gallon of wine. This is for simplicity's sake; the argument does not turn on the price chosen. In Utopia, which is better at making both goods, an hour of labour can make either a pound of cheese or half a gallon of wine. But since a pound of cheese can be traded for a gallon of wine, it makes sense for Utopia to specialise in producing cheese, and then trade some of its cheese for wine. In this way it can consume as much cheese as before and twice as much wine, or some combination of more wine and cheese.

Flatland is less efficient than Utopia at making both goods. But in Flatland too it pays to specialise. An hour of its labour can make one-sixth of a pound of cheese or one-third of a gallon of wine (which is worth one-third of a pound of cheese in the international market). So Flatland specialises in the production of wine, and trades some of its wine for cheese. Trade means that it can consume as much wine as before and twice as much cheese, or some combination of more of both.

From the assumptions this example has already made, it is possible to deduce the market-determined wage that will be paid in each country. The hourly wage in Utopia will be a pound of cheese (equal to a gallon of wine) and the wage in Flatland will be one-third of a gallon of wine (equal to one-third of a pound of cheese). In other words, the wage in Utopia will be three times the wage in Flatland. This reflects the relative price of the two goods, together with the fact that Utopia is six times more productive in cheese and 11/2 times more productive in wine.

Here is another way to think of it. Utopia is more efficient overall, so its wages are higher. This gives Flatland an opportunity to produce at lower cost, provided it specialises in wine, the good in which it has a comparative advantage (that is, a smaller absolute disadvantage). Utopia can make a gallon of wine with two hours of labour, whereas Flatland needs three – but because its wages are only one-third of Utopia's, Flatland can produce wine more cheaply. (Despite the fact that its wages are lower, Flatland cannot produce cheese more cheaply.)

Trade does not equalise incomes when productivity differs across countries, it just makes all sides better off than they would otherwise be. Moreover, trade always uncovers opportunities of this kind. Repeat, nothing central to the argument rests on the particular assumptions about price and productivity that have been used in this example.

The example has been borrowed, by the way, from an excellent textbook, *International Economics*, written by Messrs Paul Krugman (the very same) and Maurice Obstfeld. You will find it on page 22 – the principle of comparative advantage is not exactly advanced material. In parts of the real world, though, the free-trade debate still seems to be struggling with page xi (List of Contents). Krugman and Obstfeld quote with amusement an article from the *Wall Street Journal* ('The coming overthrow of free trade') which observed, "Many small countries have no comparative advantage in anything." One can imagine the writer prefacing that jewel of economic illiteracy with "Of course, we all believe in free trade, but . . .".

invest in expensive research and development, which enables these firms' productivity to continue to improve. In fields of production involving complex modern technology only very large firms can afford to keep abreast of new developments and so compete successfully in world markets.

The most obvious gain from trade is the increased choice of goods for customers. If the UK had to be self-sufficient – unable for some reason to trade with other countries – the range of goods available would be greatly diminished. For example, it is possible to produce bananas in a hothouse, but only at such high cost that few would be able to buy them. If your breakfast today included cornflakes, and tea or coffee, what would you have had instead of these imported products?

Completely free trade benefits all participants, so why then is trade restricted by **tariffs** and other measures? There are four basic reasons: ignorance, selfishness, health and strategic arguments. Ignorance of the real economic facts is possible because decisions are not taken by economists but by politicians – often on the basis of a wide variety of fallacious economic arguments. More likely is selfishness: imagine that a major employer in your locality is suffering competition from imported goods and is consequently soon to become bankrupt. The local Member of Parliament persuades the government to intervene by assisting the uncompetitive firm. What assistance is likely? A subsidy would underline the firm's uncompetitive situation and so be inadvisable, but a tariff on imports would reduce or remove the imports (often described as unfair competition) and raise prices, thus returning the firm to profitability and ensuring the jobs of its employees. But such a tariff is little different from a subsidy in that it enables an uncompetitive firm to survive. A major difference is that a subsidy is paid for by taxpayers making it obvious and unacceptable, whilst a tariff is paid for by consumers through higher prices (and reduced supplies) which seem to go unnoticed. Clearly a tariff benefits a minority at the expense of society in general. Those about to go bankrupt or lose their jobs are vociferous, whilst consumers are more dispersed and unorganized and so make no effective complaint. Consequently protective tariffs are exceedingly common. The third reason for trade barriers is to protect public health. Such trade restrictions are intended to ensure that imported canned products, for example, meet reasonable health standards, and clearly some measures of this type are justified. Finally, strategic reasons for protective tariffs or subsidies refer to a country's need to safeguard its food supply and manufacturing industries capable of producing guns, aircraft and ships in case of war; this is clearly not an economic justification.

Effects of tariff removal in a customs union

Referring to Figure 2, P_1 is the initial price in say the UK, domestic supply is Q_{S1} and consumption Q_{D1}. As a result of the removal of an import tariff after joining the customs union the price falls to P_2 and consumption rises to Q_{D2} whilst domestically produced supply falls to Q_{S2}. Clearly consumers are better off because they now consume more of the good at a lower price. The resources which had been devoted to producing $Q_{S1} - Q_{S2}$ are released for the production of other goods. Imports have increased from M_1 to M_2, the extra coming from another member or other members of the cus-

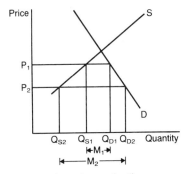

Figure 2 The consequences of a price reduction

toms union where there is a comparative advantage in the production of this good. Similarly, for some other good for which the UK has a comparative advantage, tariff removal in other member states will provide the UK with an expanded market and the production of this other good will employ the resources released by the contraction of production of the first good. **Trade creation** is the term given to such cases; clearly it benefits all members of the customs union.

Trade diversion is a potential disadvantage of joining a customs union. Remember that when the tariffs on trade between members are removed, they are replaced by common tariffs between the group and the rest of the world. So the **common external tariff** may mean that a country buys a particular good from its fellow members although it previously imported it more cheaply from a third country. It is intuitively obvious that, provided that the common external tariff adopted is not higher on average than the previous tariffs of member states which it replaces, the gains from trade creation will exceed the losses from trade diversion.

This analysis has been conducted in terms of tariffs. Clearly the gains from tariff removal are applicable to the removal of any other forms of trade barriers.

Economic integration
There are five levels of economic integration between countries. Inevitably each implies a degree of political integration.

Preference areas
These are agreements to give privileged access to certain products from specified countries. Thus, following the Ottawa Conference of 1932, a system of Imperial Preference was introduced for trade between the UK and countries of the British Empire. This involved a

reciprocal reduction of tariffs on trade between the participants, although tariffs against outsiders remained relatively high. Imperial Preference was designed to help the exports of agricultural products from the Empire to Britain, and the exports of British manufacturers to the Empire. The **Lomé convention** has since 1975 given preferential access to the Community market for some products of certain developing countries. In this instance the preferential treatment is one-way, and is regarded as a form of development aid.

Free trade areas
Here, trade in an agreed list of products occurs freely between the members of the free trade area, although members retain their independent tariffs against third countries. Such an arrangement is an attempt to gain the benefits of comparative advantage and specialization with a minimal loss of sovereignty. The political content of an agreement is limited to rules which are necessary for its fair operation. Rules of origin are the basic requirement. These prevent third-country imports into one country with a low tariff being re-exported to another member having a high tariff without paying the difference.

AT THE CROSS-ROAD

Customs union

This extends the free trade area idea to include a common external tariff against third countries. However, it involves far more political cooperation than does a free trade area. For example, the member states have to agree on the levels of tariff set and on their revision. This will obviously involve joint trade negotiations with third countries.

Common market

This adds freedom of movement for factors of production (labour and capital) to the free trade in goods and services of a customs union. Proper application of the law of comparative advantage requires that there are no distortions to competition. Consequently much common policy formulation is required so that a great deal of political cooperation is essential.

Economic and monetary union

A common market between member states having separate currencies still involves some internal trade barriers. These are transaction costs and uncertainty. The former relate to the cost of buying and selling currencies which are obviously part of any trade in goods and services. Uncertainty arises because exchange rates can alter between the time when a deal is planned and the time when it is executed, and such a change may turn profit into loss. The full exploitation of comparative advantage is only possible if there is a single currency. Thus **economic and monetary union** describes the situation when two or more countries unite their economics completely. In turn this implies political union also, for the effective control of an economy covers the money supply, taxation, the redistribution of resources – in short, all the major economic decisions undertaken by a modern state.

Expected economic benefits of the Community

As discussed in the previous chapter, the removal of tariff barriers is a necessary but not sufficient condition for free trade. The Community failed to follow up its initial removal of tariffs on internal trade with the required complementary measures, and so the promised economic benefits did not materialize to any great extent. The **Single European Act** was passed in 1986 to remedy this situation. It aims at the removal of *all* trade barriers by the end of 1992.

As the accompanying article from *Europe in Figures* indicates, the Single European Market is estimated to make the EC better off to the tune of ECU125 milliard to ECU190 milliard (£84 billion to £127 billion) per year. Such figures are difficult to comprehend, but percentages give a sense of perspective: according to the Commission, Community GDP is estimated to increase by about 4.5 per cent and employment by 1.5 per cent whilst inflation will be slightly reduced. These are the 'static' benefits – those that should be achieved within the first few years. In the long term the dynamic benefit is an expected increase of about one percentage point in the rate of economic growth.

The Single European Act

In December 1985, the European Council (the Heads of State or Government) meeting in Luxembourg, decided to give new impetus to European integration by drawing up a 'Single European Act', which was signed in February 1986 and came into force on 1 July 1987.

The Single Act is a new Treaty which modifies and supplements the Treaties of Paris and Rome (which established the three European Communities: ECSC, EEC, Euratom). Its aim is to bring the Community into line with the needs of the 1990s and to shape it into one large economic unit, a truly frontierless internal market with a population of 320 million: the biggest in the world.

Acting on the fact that Europe's lack of integration is proving expensive to the citizens of the Community (costing between ECU 125 and 190 thousand million per year according to studies carried out by the Commission), the decision-makers in the Member States have decided to do everything possible to create, by 1 January 1993, a 'vast single market'. Citizens of the Twelve will be able to live and work in the country of their choice, regardless of what job they do. Tourists and travellers will be able to travel without frontier checks and use their credit cards in all the countries of the Community. Businesses will have a far wider market, leading to greater profitability from investment and the creation of employment – in short, an area in which there will be total freedom of movement for persons, goods and capital.

Source: *Europe in Figures*, 1989/90 edn, Eurostat

```
┌─────────────────────────────────────────────────────────────┐
│                        KEY WORDS                             │
│  Law of Comparative          Economic integration           │
│    Advantage                 Reciprocal reduction           │
│  Economies of size           Lomé convention                │
│  Dynamic process             Economic and monetary          │
│  Tariffs                       union                        │
│  Trade creation              Single European Act            │
│  Trade diversion             Static benefits                │
│  Common external tariff      Dynamic benefit                │
└─────────────────────────────────────────────────────────────┘
```

Reading list

Lipsey, R. and Harbury, C., *First Principles of Economics*, Weidenfeld, 1988 (on trade and comparative advantage).

Eckert, R.D. and Leftwich, R.H., *The Price System and Resource Allocation*, 10th edn, 1988, p.286 (on economies of size).

Essay topics

1. In what ways do customs unions or free trade areas affect the gains from trade? (University of Oxford Delegacy of Local Examinations, 1989)
2. Explain the difference between a 'free trade area', a 'customs union' and a 'common market'. To what extent does the European Community match the above theoretical models? (University of Cambridge Local Examinations Syndicate, 1989)
3. Explain how countries gain from specialization and international trade. Why then do countries restrict free international trade? (University of Cambridge Local Examinations Syndicate, 1988)

Data Response Question 1
Bilateral Trade

This task concerns the following extracts which are based on news reports broadcast on UK television and radio during 1990 and 1991. Read them carefully, then answer the following questions.

1. In the eighteenth century, Adam Smith attacked the views of the Mercantilists, who believed that all trade was for the benefit of the 'mother country'. What evidence is there in the extracts to suggest that popular opinion is still largely mercantilist?
2. Trade does not take place between *nations* as such, but instead takes place between firms and households, and producers and

consumers. Bearing this in mind, does a balance of trade deficit actually matter?

3. Why is it often assumed that a deficit is necessarily bad and a surplus necessarily good? Are there grounds for thinking the opposite? Justify your answers.

4. Do you agree with economists such as Smith, Hume and Ricardo, who argued that trade would benefit all countries, or with the mercantilist view that one country can only benefit at the expense of others?

... **The Japanese Ministry of Trade is under fire from the West, because while imports into Japan remain at less than 50% of exports, the Japanese market is effectively closed to Western business people by a host of bureaucratic regulations. Japan remains a free importer of commodities, exploiting the cost savings to give better profit margins on the consumer goods made from them. But as far as mass-produced consumer goods are concerned, the trade ministry determined to fight its corner rather than change its ways.**

... **The lamb war with France took a tasty turn yesterday when French farmers were accused of hijacking a British lorry and burning alive its cargo of sheep. We might expect to see once again such lurid headlines as 'Hop off you frogs' which have been used to indicate the strength of feeling on this issue, at least among some elements of the British tabloid press.**

... **During her American visit, Mrs Thatcher spoke out on Europe for the first time since leaving office as Prime Minister. She expressed fears that the European Community would become dominated by its most successful member, Germany. Her supporters point out that Britain's deficit with Germany is larger than its deficit with Japan.**

Chapter Three

Competition and the Community

'Before the Single European Act it would have taken an accountant 50 years to qualify and requalify in each member country so as to be able to audit in each country!'

This chapter examines how free competition is to be achieved – it involves much more than the simple step of removing tariff barriers on internal trade. As trade with the rest of the world is more important to the EC than to any other major bloc or country, it is appropriate also to discuss here the attitude to competition in world markets.

Internal competition

It should be remembered that a common market involves the free movement of goods, services, capital and labour between a group of countries. Emphasis is to be laid on the word *free*, both here and in the term free competition. Only in a free market can comparative advantage, specialization and concomitant economies of size be attained.

Economies of size in many fields of industrial production can be gained only by very large firms, much larger than those existing within the EC when it was formed. This implies either the growth of some firms, and the demise of their internal competitors, or their growth by merger and acquisition regardless of member state boundaries. Unfortunately the arrival of 'European firms' large enough to compete successfully in world markets with the largest American and Japanese firms requires the removal of national legal, technical and fiscal barriers by **harmonization** (an important Community term) implying the replacement of national by community-wide laws, standards and taxes.

Harmonization in the industrial field has turned out to be extremely slow and difficult – this is one of the factors behind the introduction of the Single European Act (SEA) already mentioned, and discussed in detail below. The only significant industrial activity undertaken at Community level before the SEA was its assistance to

25

On harmonization

'There was one card I particularly resented sending. It was to the EEC Agriculture Commissioner in Brussels. I would rather have sent him a redundancy notice. He's even worse than his colleagues, and I can't speak any worse of anybody than that. He's the fool who has forced through the plan to standardise the Eurosausage. By the end of next year we'll be waving goodbye to the good old British sausage, and we'll be forced to accept some foreign muck like salami or bratwurst in its place.

'Of course, they can't actually *stop* us eating the British sausage. But they can stop us calling it a sausage. It seems that it's got to be called *the Emulsified High-Fat Offal Tube*. And I was forced to swallow it. I mean, it is a perfectly accurate description of the thing, but not awfully appetising. And it doesn't exactly trip lightly off the tongue. It sticks in the throat, as a matter of fact. There's going to be frightful trouble over it.

'But it's my job to implement EEC regulations. And, in exchange for getting a new deal on farm prices and on Britain's reduced contribution to the community budget, a concession had to be made. The PM didn't seem to mind, nor did the FO, nor did Agriculture – presumably because I'm the one who is to be landed with trying to sell this to the British people. It could ruin my career.'

Extract from YES PRIME MINISTER by Jonathan Lynn and Anthony Jay

---

declining industries. Steel is the major example. The European steel industry suffered from chronic excess capacity and lack of international competitiveness. Its reduction in size and its modernization have been coordinated by the Community, greatly assisted by the existence of the European Coal and Steel Community, which provided the necessary mechanisms.

Removing tariffs on internal trade is a necessary but not sufficient condition for free internal trade. There is a plethora of **non-tariff barriers** (NTBs) and state aids, *inter alia,* which effectively prevent or greatly reduce trade. NTBs include different technical standards and complex documentation. At the extreme, the manufacturer of a product might have to produce it in twelve different versions to satisfy different national criteria, and similarly provide different documentation for each member state, involving several languages. There are many other ways in which internal trade may be distorted, and the one which attracts most attention is state aid. Helping industries through the provision of production subsidies, artificially low interest rates, research and development expenditures and so on, may be legitimate (though economically dubious) government activities, but if practised differently by the individual member states competition will obviously be distorted. The Commission has struggled to remove the many distortions to competition which exist in the Community. Progress has been slow because of the reluctance of member states to stop helping their own national producers. Before we turn to transport and energy as significant examples of these problems, look at Table 4 – the growth of internal trade indicates that although progress has been slow it has been substantial.

Table 4 EC member states' trade with other members as a percentage of total trade in 1958 and 1987

	Imports		Exports	
	1958	1987	1958	1987
Belgium/Luxembourg	56	70	55	74
Denmark	60	54	59	50
West Germany	36	53	38	54
Greece	54	61	51	67
Spain	32	57	47	61
France	28	65	31	62
Ireland	69	71	82	74
Italy	30	58	35	57
Netherland	50	62	58	75
Portugal	53	66	39	72
United Kingdom	22	49	22	50
Total EC(12)	35	59	37	59

Source: *European Economy* 42, 1989

Transport policy

A common transport policy is called for in the Treaty of Rome. Transport costs can contribute substantially to the total costs of goods. If they can be reduced by improvements in the efficiency of the industry the effect would be similar to a reduction of tariff barriers. However, the primary reason for the Treaty's requirement for a common policy was widespread intervention in member states. In general, intervention tended to encourage exports and hinder imports and could be used by individual member states to distort competition in favour of their own producers.

Member states have been extremely reluctant to give up their national transport policies. Indeed, in 1982 the Commission took the Council of Ministers to the Court of Justice for not fulfilling their Treaty obligation to introduce a common policy. The Court agreed with this complaint and in a 1985 judgement told them in effect to get on with it. The most restrictive element of national policies was that lorries had to be licensed to carry goods, but the licences were only valid in the country of issue. So a lorry might be able to take a load from one member state to another but would be unable to pick up a load for the return journey. Some liberalization has taken place since the 1985 judgement, but the development of a comprehensive policy still seems some way off. Probably the only fragments of common policy to have come to public notice are in road haulage: the introduction of standard maximum driving hours and rest periods led to the use of the tachograph and the agreement on uniform axle weights and dimensions for lorries. UK lorry drivers called the tachograph 'the spy in the cab' and UK citizens in general worried that 'continental juggernauts' would destroy our beautiful towns and villages – a practical example of the difficulty of 'harmonization'.

Energy policy

There are similarities between transport and energy in that the latter can also, as a result of different national policies, distort competition in the internal market. However the EEC Treaty does not call for a common energy policy although one is clearly desirable, and the situation is complicated by the fact that coal is governed by the ECSC and nuclear energy by Euratom, leaving other energy sources to the EEC by default. Much Community-level action has been to assist in the rundown of the coal industry. Oil has been displacing coal as the major energy source, but its supplies are imported (except for the UK and Netherlands) and are subject to great political uncertainties. Consequently the EC has a policy of greater self-sufficiency, which in the face of declining coal production implies energy conservation and more nuclear power. The former has become a main plank of policy, but expanding nuclear power has not proved feasible in the face of substantial opposition from a public worried about the long-term problems of nuclear fission. The Community also has an agreement whereby member states maintain emergency oil stocks sufficient for 90 days of normal consumption. Alternative energy sources are the subject of very significant Community-level research. Early results suggest that wind, wave and solar power seem likely to contribute little to future energy requirements. Hopes are focussed on the Joint European Torus

(JET). This seeks to harness the energy released by nuclear fusion, which in marked contrast to nuclear fission (the process used in nuclear power stations) does not produce harmful radiation and residues. JET is a most ambitious technological development, extremely expensive, particularly in terms of scientific resources, yet promising virtually unlimited supplies of cheap 'clean' energy in the future – possibly in 50 years' time. Such a long-term and expensive project would have been beyond the resources of individual members, and its existence indicates the potential advantage of a union of states.

Despite the fundamental importance of energy supplies in industrial countries there is no common energy policy. The items discussed above are piecemeal interventions only. Doubtless the Commission will attempt to develop a more comprehensive policy.

Competition policy

The discussion so far has focussed on national government policies, but private firms can also indulge in practices which distort competition. Price fixing and market sharing cartels are the prime examples. National governments have long had their own measures to combat cartels. The Community leaves the control of cartels within member states to the members themselves unless there is an appreciable effect on trade between members. In the latter case the Commission has wide powers to prohibit agreements intended to prevent, restrict or distort competition within the common market. Similarly, the Commission can prevent a firm which has a 'dominant position' (i.e. a monopoly) from abusing that position. Having a dominant position is itself permitted – indeed the Community wishes to see more very large European firms capable of competing with the largest foreign firms in the world market; it is only the abuse of dominance which is prohibited. Control over mergers and acquisitions which might give rise to a dominant position was agreed in 1989 – see the article on page 30 reproduced from the *Financial Times* of 22 December 1989.

The Single European Act

In Chapter 1, this Act (SEA) was described as the 'relaunching' of the Community. It was necessitated by the effect of non-tariff barriers (NTBs) preventing the free movement of goods, services, capital and labour within the Community, and the slow progress made towards the removal of these barriers under the unanimity system of decision making. In 1985 the EC heads of government committed themselves to creating a single European market by the end of 1992.

EC ministers agree common merger policy

Peter Guilford, Brussels

Ministers of the European Community have given unanimous backing to a common merger policy empowering the European Commission to block or authorize most of the biggest mergers that take place in Britain.

Mr John Redwood, Under-Secretary for Corporate Affairs, finally lifted the Government's long-standing opposition to the measures during a meeting of EC internal market ministers in Brussels yesterday, after making a telephone call to London to secure Mrs Thatcher's approval.

In return, he won a commitment from Sir Leon Brittan, European commissioner for competition, to issue a statement by next March on removing all remaining technical barriers which thwart British takeover bids elsewhere in the EC.

As many as 50 of the largest company mergers in Europe could now be controlled by the Brussels competition authorities each year. The City claims four out of every five of these involve a British company. The commission claims that up to 15 of the biggest cases annually would be lifted from the hands of the Monopolies and Mergers Commission.

Sir Leon hailed it as "unquestionably an historic breakthrough for the Community in the context of the single European market. There can be no internal market without a common competition policy."

A special adviser on merger policy to Sir Leon claimed later that mergers involving BAT and Consolidated Gold-Fields, and GEC and Plessey could have fallen within the new rules.

The deal ends 16 years of protracted negotiations, and will have a profound impact on industry, giving British companies with ambitions to expand throughout Europe a clearer picture of how and by whom their merger plans will be judged.

Under the new regulation, all mergers with a worldwide aggregate turnover each year of more than five billion Ecu (£3.6 billion) need prior clearance from Brussels. Smaller mergers – or larger ones where each company has over two-thirds of its Community turnover in one and the same member state – must apply to the MMC or equivalent European bodies for authorization.

Even large companies incorporated outside the EC would be controlled by Brussels if a merger between them threatened to distort competition on the Community market. For this to happen, they must generate at least 250 million ECU of their annual business in Europe.

The regulation will enter into force in nine months time. The commission expects to clear most mergers after one month, but may suspend others for a further four months until taking a final decision.

It was agreed that individual governments may seek permission from Brussels to vet mergers above the five billion ECU threshold if they fear an adverse impact on a "distinct" market within their territory. Brussels may refuse such permission.

The commission has effectively renounced all existing powers under the Treaty of Rome's competition rules over mergers below five billion ECU, unless explicitly asked by national governments to intervene.

Up to three times as many mergers could come under commission scrutiny in four years from now, when the five billion ECU threshold is reviewed by EC governments. A commission spokesman said: "We will definitely push to have this reduced to two billion ECU."

Britain is expected to oppose such a move.

The SEA amends the Treaty of Rome, and came into force on 1 July 1987. Since then NTBs have been progressively removed over a wide field, decisions being greatly speeded by the adoption of a system of majority voting (see Chapter 1).

Purchasing by governments and other public bodies accounts for about 15 per cent of Community GDP. Traditionally such purchases have been almost exclusively from national suppliers and contractors. As part of the 1992 programme such **public procurement** has been the subject of new directives which aim to ensure that all companies in the Community have a fair chance of tendering for contracts. These directives prohibit discriminatory specifications and complex tendering procedures, force major contracts to be advertised at Community level with reasonable time limits for bids to be received. Purchasers must be prepared to justify their rejection of bids, and complaints can be taken to the Court. Electricity generating equipment and railway equipment are typical of the sectors which will be most affected by the new rules. Traditionally each national public authority favoured its national champions, with the consequence that intra-Community trade was very small, price differences between member states were substantial and rates of capacity utilization were low. Clearly, because the potential economies of size in these sectors are very large, the new rules will lead to a major restructuring through mergers, concentration, and closure of plants.

In the long term the Community aims to harmonize **business laws** and **technical standards** but this is a very slow process. In the short term some pragmatic changes have been introduced to free markets from legal and technical NTBs. Thus, a standard Single European Document has been introduced to accompany goods being sent across the Community, replacing a plethora of complex different national documents. Most important on the technical front is the principle that what is acceptable in one member state must be acceptable in others. For example, in Germany, regulations insist that beer must be made from water, malt and hops only; all other additives are prohibited. The Court of Justice has ruled that not withstanding this, the Germans must permit the import of beers from other member states – additives and all – provided that such beers meet with the national standards in their countries of origin. This attitude is obviously going to permit the free movement of goods long before European standards can be agreed. It also applies in general to services and the professions. Before the SEA, it would have taken an accountant 50 years to qualify and requalify in each member country so as to be able to audit in each country!

Although much progress has been made towards the completion of the single market by the end of 1992, some significant problems remain. Indeed, progress has been rapid partly because the easier NTBs have been dealt with first, leaving the more controversial ones until the end. The harmonization of rates of tax and excise duty is proving to be a particularly intractable problem, although members have committed themselves to this in principle as one of the provisions of the Single European Act. Progress is hindered by the fact that all fiscal decisions are still subject to unanimity in the Council of Ministers. Differences in rates are considerable and they can be major distortions of competition. Excise duties are a ready illustration: wine in the UK attracts a high rate of duty (most wine being imported) compared with beer (mainly UK produced). As the accompanying article (reproduced from *The Economist* of 13 January 1990) explains, such difficulties are delaying a 'true' single market.

Single - market phooey

Europe's 1992 plans are still threatened by tax inspectors

Do you imagine post-1992 Europeans being able to send things by post throughout the European Community as easily as within their own countries? You could be wrong. Do you imagine that small companies will be able to sell directly by mail-order to customers across the EC, as they do in America? You are certainly wrong. Do you imagine that sales of goods and services between EC countries will soon be indistinguishable from sales within a country? Wrong again. By such simple yardsticks, Europe's much-vaunted "single market" is set to remain a fraud.

Tax has always promised to be the Achilles heel of the 1992 project.

Europe's rates of value-added tax and excise duties differ too much to survive a truly open market. The way governments insist on collecting VAT on the full value of something acquired on their territory – even if most of its value was added elsewhere in Europe – makes the market much harder to unify. These dangers have long been obvious. They have provoked more shuffling of feet, staring out of windows and glazing of ministerial eyeballs than any of the 278 other measures needed to make the single market work.

Indifference is becoming deceit. The official news from Brussels is that heartening progress is being made towards a Europe without fiscal frontier controls. Hardly. It is still uncertain whether people will be free to take as much as they want across European frontiers. There is no agreement on what to do, or not to do, about differences in excise and VAT rates. The only thing agreed is that there should be no checks of tax-papers at frontiers on commercial traffic across the EC: such checks will involve buyers and sellers in extra paperwork instead.

Governments are removing border controls by devising bureaucratic substitutes for them, not by removing the underlying need for them.

Finance ministers know this, but have postponed until 1996, at the earliest, a fraud-proof VAT system that would indeed allow Europe to be a single market. Part of the problem is that the new tax commissioner, Mrs Christiane Scrivener, has been too much of a pushover for national governments where her predecessor, Lord Cockfield, was maddeningly dogmatic. But the failure of both styles points to the deeper problem: Europe's governments cannot face the fiscal consequences of the market they say they want.

Mail order is a good example of this backsliding. Many American companies have prospered by direct-selling across America via the order-form or telephone number included in their advertisements: Apple Computer came out of its Californian garage that way. The EC governments will insist that mail-order sales involve the appointment of a sales agent in each country to levy that country's rate of tax. Tell that to Europe's garage-based entrepreneurs. As for gifts-by-mail, they will have to carry a sticker telling local tax inspectors that they are not worth too much. How much remains unclear.

Let VAT do its elegant best
At the least, governments should waive the "tax at destination" rules in both these cases – which is effectively what American states do. But as governments wrestle with such problems of tax-leakage, they are coming to realise that the only workable way forward is for Europe's VAT system to treat the EC as one market. This is not merely because having a special VAT regime for "exports" and "imports" within a single market is absurd, but mainly because that regime kills one of VAT's best features. The elegance of VAT is that it is self-policing: proof of a seller's collection of tax is evidence of the buyer's right to a tax deduction. It is the breaking of this chain at national frontiers that makes border controls or bureaucratic substitutes necessary.

Governments should allow VAT paid anywhere in the EC to be VAT-deductible everywhere else. They should then use a simple settlement system to steer the accustomed tax flows to each exchequer. They have already conceded the need for this in principle, but would rather delay fiscal 1992 until after 1996, without saying so. Their ruse has been spotted.

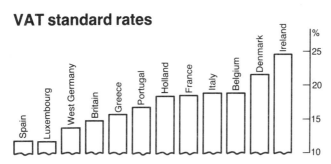

VAT standard rates

Spain, Luxembourg, West Germany, Britain, Greece, Portugal, Holland, France, Italy, Belgium, Denmark, Ireland

%
25
20
15
10

External trade

The Community accounts for about 20 per cent of world trade and is the world's largest trading group. As Table 5 shows, EC exports to the world market far exceed those of the USA and Japan. External trade is about 10 per cent of Community GDP. Clearly no discussion of Community competition is complete without some consideration of the EC's position in world markets.

Table 5 Relative importance of EC in world trade 1987

	Imports	Exports
	(Mrd ECU)	
European Community	338	339
USA	352	219
Japan	130	199
World	1704	1704
EC internal trade	491	491

Sources: *Eurostatistics*, vol. 7, 1990; *European Economy*, vol. 42, 1989

In 1947 the leading trading nations signed the General Agreement on Tariffs and Trade (**GATT**). This sought to avoid the protectionism of the 1930s which had greatly exacerbated the worldwide depression. Its main aim was to reduce trade barriers, though it excluded agriculture and services. Its crucial principle is the **most-favoured-nation clause;** under this, a country agreeing a tariff reduction to one country is obliged to offer the same reduction to all GATT members. How can the EC countries with zero internal tariffs and a common external tariff against third countries belong to GATT? The rules exempt customs unions and free trade areas from this non-discrimination rule provided that their formation does not raise the tariffs of the new trade group to a level greater on average than the previous tariffs of the individual members. It is also permissible to offer reduced tariffs on a discriminatory basis to developing countries.

In Article 110 of the Treaty of Rome the Community states its intention of contributing to 'the harmonious development of world trade, the progressive abolition of restrictions on international exchanges and the lowering of customs barriers'. To date the Community has two main discriminatory agreements: one is for reciprocal free trade in industrial products with the European Free Trade Area; the other – the Lomé Convention – offers non-reciprocal tariff preferences for most non-agricultural goods and preferential access for some food products. The Lomé Convention covers 66 African, Caribbean and Pacific (ACP) countries, mostly the ex-colonies of EC members. In addition to trade preferences it also provides aid for the ACP countries with special funds to stabilize their export earnings, and a European Development Fund to finance development projects.

From time to time GATT members enter a round of international negotiations to try to liberalize trade. As the EC has a common trade policy the Commission represents the Community, though its agreements have to be ratified by the Council of Ministers. Successive rounds of negotiations in GATT since 1947 give the impression that trade barriers have been progressively reduced since tariffs have certainly fallen to low levels. The truth is that their place tends to have been taken by NTBs. Two examples underline the point. The **Multi-fibre Arrangements** (between developed-country textile importers, notably EC, USA and Japan, and developing-country exporters) place quantitative restrictions on trade. Similarly, the EC's large trade deficit with Japan has led to the imposition of **Voluntary Export Restraints** (VERs) on a wide range of goods such as motor cars and electronic items. Such quantitative restrictions have become common. In 1985 it was agreed to launch a new round of trade negotiations, the **Uruguay Round** (since this is where the initial conference was held), to be completed by the end of 1990. As this round was to include agriculture in addition to tariffs and NTBs, it is not surprising that progress has been slow. The main protagonists are the USA and the EC. The former has an enormous international trade deficit, not helped by the fact that one of its major exports – food – has to compete in world markets with the heavily subsidized exports of the Community (see the next chapter). So the USA wants to see the Community's agricultural policy remodelled to remove these dumped surpluses and is willing to reform its own system of protecting agriculture. The success of the Uruguay Round hinges largely on the agricultural problem. At the time of writing (autumn 1990) the prospects of further trade liberalization look poor despite the fact that freer trade would be in the interests of all.

KEY WORDS

Harmonization
Non-tariff barriers
Liberalization
Dominant position
Single European Act
Public procurement
Business laws
Technical standards

GATT
Most-favoured-nation
  clause
Multi-fibre Arrangements
Voluntary Export
  Restraints
Uruguay Round

Reading list

Begg, D., Fischer, S. and Dornbusch, R., *Economics,* 2nd edn, pp. 697–704, McGraw-Hill.

Bennett, P. and Cave, M., *Competition Policy,* Heinemann Educational, chap. 3, 1991.

Cook, M. and Healey, N., *Current Topics in International Economics,* chap. 4, Anforme, 1990.

McDonald, F., 'Completing the internal market', *Economics, The Journal of the Economics Association,* Spring 1988.

McKenzie, G. and Venables, T., 'Economics of 1992', *Economic Review,* May 1989.

Symons, E. and Walker, E., 'Fiscal harmonisation in the EEC', *Economic Review,* May 1990.

Essay topics

1. Discuss whether or not it is possible to give an accurate measure of living standards in an economy. Explain the effect that the creation of the single European market is likely to have on living standards in the UK. (Joint Matriculation Board, 1990)
2. In relation to intra-EC trade discuss the following: (a) harmonization; (b) NTBs; (c) VAT; (d) mergers.
3. Examine the arguments for unrestricted international trade. In the light of these arguments, how could you justify the imposition of tariffs on US goods by the European Community? (University of London School Examinations Board, 1990)
4. Explain the theory of comparative advantage. Is the theory of any use in explaining the pattern of world trade? (University of London School Examinations Board, 1989)
5. 'If the theory of comparative advantage points to the benefit of international specialisation there is no basis for government inter-

ference with trade.' Discuss. (University of London School
Examinations Board, 1988)
6. Will the creation of a single European market in 1992 lead to
fundamental changes in Britain's economic relationship with the
European Community? (Oxford and Cambridge Schools
Examination Board, 1990)

Data Response Question 2

In 1988 the European Community imposed a special levy on the
import of Japanese dot matrix printers, amounting to 33.4 per cent.
This spurred the Japanese manufacturers into a public outrage. On 8
September 1988, one of the leading manufacturers, Epson, published a large advertisement in national newspapers, the text of
which is reproduced here. Read the Epson case, and then answer the
following questions. This task is based on an examination question
set by the University of Cambridge Schools Examination Board in
1990.

1. Explain what is meant by 'dumping'.
2. (a) What evidence was used by the European Community to
determine that the Seiko Epson Corporation was dumping its
products in the European market?
(b) On what grounds did the Seiko Epson Corporation reject this
evidence?
3. What are the likely effects of the 33.4 per cent levy on each of the
following? (i) UK business consumers. (ii) The Seiko Epson
Corporation's manufacturing operations in Europe. (iii) The operations of other Japan-based manufacturers of printers.
4. In the light of this particular case, *evaluate* the arguments for and
against import levies.

'We acted like any good business should'

On May 27th, 1988, the members of a special Commission investigating
claims by European printer manufacturers into alleged Japanese 'dumping'
delivered their verdict
   Guilty.
   The price to be paid? A stiff levy on Japanese dot matrix printers.
   That includes us. Epson. The world's leading producers of printers and,
facing a levy of 33.4%, now a rather bemused spokesman for the Japanese
printer industry.

37

Maybe you think Japan deserves levies. Or maybe the whole thing seems irrelevant to you.

If so, it may surprise you to know that 67% of the UK business community polled by MORI (Market & Opinion Research International) were against the imposition of levies recognising that it would increase their costs.

What's at stake here should deeply concern you if you believe there's any kind of relationship between Free Trade and successful business.

It's our opinion that the levy is unjust. It's been arrived at on the basis of calculations, statistics and reasoning which are demonstrably wrong.

But what's worse for all of us in business, whether in the East or the West, is that the levy is counter productive.

It may well harm the very industry it's designed to protect. And if it breeds more legislation like it, you may find you rue the day you missed your chance to prevent it spreading no matter what business you're in.

Again, these are things you might expect us to say. But we're not objecting to this levy just so that we can be seen to put up some kind of a fight.

We are fundamentally opposed to it and, with respect, would ask you to listen to our case.

An unfair comparison

Most Japanese companies (ourselves included) make healthy profits on their overseas trade – not something you achieve by selling below cost.

So the Commission had to look elsewhere for this elusive proof of dumping.

They looked at the price Japanese printers are sold for to dealers in Japan and compared this with the price dealers in Europe buy them for.

But this was not a 'like for like' comparison.

All of Epson's European costs, right down to postage stamps, were deducted, whereas in Japan only marketing and selling costs were considered.

Small wonder they found a discrepancy . . . .

A different market

Equally, in its deliberations, the Commission compared European and Japanese manufacturers as if we were all competing for the same market.

This is patently not so.

Europe chose several years ago to concentrate on the niche market of high price, heavy duty printers.

Japan (and Epson in particular) chose to develop the high volume, IBM compatible market in Europe.

Quite freely and independently, we both went our separate ways.

It seems absurd to us that European manufacturers can now complain that we are stealing a market from them which they never chose to be a part of in the first place.

And the Commission tell us that to decrease the dumping margin, and thus the levy, all we have to do is increase our prices in Europe!

Where will it all end?

There's even talk now of extending the levy to include components, not just finished products, apparently to punish us for having brought manufacturing jobs to Europe.

Ironically, if our manufacturing base were Korea or Taiwan and we imported our printers, to sell them at much lower prices, we would be unaffected.

The European Commission talks about Japanese manufacturing plants destroying jobs in Europe. But these are jobs Europe never had. The new jobs created have in fact been transferred directly from Japan.

Isn't that what the Commission wanted?

The fact remains, because we have invested in Europe, we are to be penalised.

This in the face of our open commitment to finding components within Europe whenever possible.

These things can't happen overnight.

Our products sell on quality and reliability. Given a reasonable amount of time, we will find that quality in Europe and gladly incorporate it into our products.

At the moment the duty of 33.4% is only provisional. But it's due to be made definite in November.

We think it penalises us unfairly for being an astute, successful business. We also agree with those who call it 'a tax on users'.

If we are to make Free Trade something more than a slogan in the European Market, we should join in exposing the levy for what it really is, a *"measure so transparently inept that it might just help to discredit Europe's fondness for self-destructive trade policy"* (*The Economist* 4/6/88).

Chapter Four

The Common Agricultural Policy

Judged by any criterion of economics or commonsense this policy is an expensive disaster, yet its reform appears to be beyond the wit of politicians. If Alice had observed an agricultural policy Through The Looking Glass, this might have been it.

When the Community (of Six) began in 1958 about 20 per cent of its population was employed in agriculture, making this by far the largest industry. Each member state had its own agricultural policy. Harmonizing these policies was essential, otherwise they would result in different food prices in different countries, and this would distort competition – because manufacturing wages are influenced by food prices. The need to develop a common agricultural policy is stated in Article 3 of the Treaty of Rome. It is the first common policy mentioned, underlining the importance attached to it. The need to unify existing disparate policies is obvious, but why were agricultural policies needed anyway?

Reasons for agricultural policies
Returning to medieval times, most of the population were occupied by agriculture. The process of economic development involves the transfer of much of this labour force to other activities. Necessarily, the first requirement is for an increase in labour productivity in agriculture, so that some labour can be released. In practice land productivity increased along with that of labour, as food production increased, and food prices declined. Consequently the returns to agricultural resources in general declined. So resources were reallocated from agriculture to more profitable uses. History demonstrates that labour is persuaded to leave agriculture only slowly, resulting in incomes that are persistently below those of other occupations. In the twentieth century, low incomes for such a large sector of the economy came to be considered as inequitable, and so became the focus for government intervention.

Another economic reason for intervention is that agricultural prices are inherently unstable in a free market. **Price elasticities** of demand for food products are low – because consumption of food means physical consumption, and once people are full a reduction in prices will not persuade them to eat much more. Neither will a rise in price greatly reduce their desire to eat. Imagine that the price elasticity of demand for potatoes is –0.1, in a particular year the yield of potatoes is low owing to drought and marketed output is reduced by 5 per cent. Clearly potato prices will rise and farmers can do nothing about it; extra potatoes can only be produced next year (i.e. the supply is perfectly inelastic in the short run). How much will prices rise? – with these data, 50 per cent. Thus, if the price elasticity of demand is low, which it is for most agricultural products, small changes in outputs cause relatively large changes in prices. Such unstable prices fail to tell producers what consumers really want. Some action to stabilize prices is therefore likely to result in an improvement in **economic efficiency.**

There is also a strategic argument for intervention in agriculture. A secure food supply is an essential element of policy for any government and is neglected at a country's peril. The UK discovered this in the early years of this century. Comparative advantage had been followed resulting in the UK exporting manufactures and importing food – a sound economic policy which seemed safe as there had been peace in Europe for a hundred years. When the First World War began three-quarters of the flour in British bread was imported!

The Common Agricultural Policy

The aims of the policy as stated in Article 39 may be summarized as follows:

(a) to increase productivity;
(b) to raise farm incomes;
(c) to stabilize markets;
(d) to assure the availability of supplies;
(e) to ensure reasonable prices for consumers.

Although the Treaty of Rome does not make it clear, the fundamental objective is the raising of farm incomes and we now turn to the method of achieving this.

Price support

The Community decided that farmers' incomes were too low because their product prices were too low, and so it designed a policy to raise prices. Figure 3 relates to the situation in the 1960s when the policy was introduced. The supply and demand curves relate to

Community farmers and consumers. Free trade would result in a Community price level of WP, standing for World Price. At this price Q_{S1} and Q_{D1} would be produced and consumed respectively, the difference being imported. The Community decided to raise the wholesale price to TP (**Target Price**). At this price farmers expand production to Q_{S2} and consumption declines to Q_{D2}. Cheap imports are prevented from undermining the target price by a **variable import levy** (VIL) which raises WP to at least TP. The effects of the policy are to raise prices substantially – TP is much higher than WP – for the benefit of farmers. Prices are also stabilized, for if WP varies, the variable import levy is altered to compensate, thus keeping TP virtually constant. Consumers are worse off since they have to pay higher prices for less consumption; indeed the area ABCE (price difference times consumption) is an **implicit food tax.** Area FBCG (variable import levy times quantity imported) represents the revenue collected on imports which reduces the need for other taxation. The policy evidently transfers income from food consumers to farmers and taxpayers. Of course countries supplying imports are worse off as their market is diminished.

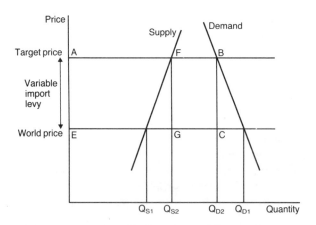

Figure 3 The *intended* operation of CAP price supports

This support policy ignored time and the changes which it brings. Although the Community demand for food has not changed much, since the population has been almost constant, supplies have continually expanded under the spur of technological progress, encouraged by the artificially high level of prices. So in Figure 4 the supply curve has moved to the right, and at the administered price TP, EC production exceeds consumption even in the absence of imports. Originally the policy raised prices by reducing imports; when imports are zero as in this figure, what is to stop price falling below TP to the level indicated by the intersection of demand and supply? – an **intervention system**. It was realized from the beginning that for many products a post-harvest glut would force market prices below TP even without imports. An intervention agency in each member state was formed to buy and store produce at intervention prices –set a little below target prices. Later in the season there would be seasonal shortages permitting the sale of the post-harvest surpluses. But the situation in Figure 4 has become the rule: supplies have increased so much that surpluses are 'normal' instead of seasonal and they are purchased and stored with little likelihood of future release on to the Community markets. These surpluses have become known popularly as butter, beef and cereals mountains and wine lakes. Other products are also in surplus: the EC has had vegetable oil lakes and dried currant mountains for example, but these have not so far captured the attention of journalists or the general public. Comparing Figures 3 and 4, the major change is from net imports to surpluses. What becomes of the latter?

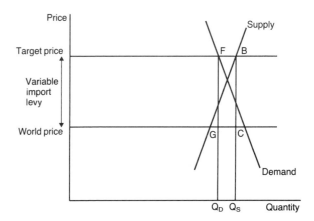

Figure 4 CAP price support in practice (cf Figure 3)

Most surpluses are exported with the aid of subsidies. To make this possible export subsidies equal to TP minus WP are necessary to enable traders to sell in world markets at world prices. Clearly there is still a transfer of income from consumers to farmers, but now taxpayers have to pay for the removal of surpluses. Third countries supplying food to the world market are disadvantaged by the 'dumping' (i.e. selling abroad below cost) of EC surpluses on their markets. On the other hand many food importers are getting marvellous bargains.

Soviet bloc picks up a £1 bn bargain

The EEC last year sold more than seven million tonnes of cereals to Russia for £785 million, as well as 162,000 tonnes of butter to a value of £137 million, both at knock-down prices.

Libya received 461,000 tonnes of EEC grain and 54,000 tonnes of skimmed milk also at subsidized rates.

The main Soviet bloc importers of EEC food–stuffs – Russia, Poland, Bulgaria and East Germany – did bargain basement business with Brussels to the tune of more than £1 billion with Libya and other North African states – Algeria, Tunisia,

Morocco and Egypt – close behind with more than £800 million worth.

But even these large-scale cut-price deals have barely dented the EEC food mountains, and the failure of EEC farm ministers this week to agree on a policy for disposal of the surpluses leaves the Commission keen to conclude further deals, including a sale of 100,000 tonnes of butter to Moscow through M. Jean Baptiste Doumeng, the French Communist trader. The secret subsidy in this deal is said to be as much as three-quarters of the official intervention price.

Source: *The Times*, 28 March 1986

It should be noted that the price policy does nothing to make farming competitive in world terms. Indeed it accepts that European farming is uncompetitive and protects farmers from competition, which ensures that they never will become competitive. The difference in price levels between the Community and world markets has been so large that fraud has become widespread, and reputably the source of much income for the Mafia and the IRA!

How to make a million

Two cargoes of corn, weighing 20,000 tons, which were smuggled into Greece have led to the Greek authorities being found guilty of one of the biggest European frauds to have been uncovered recently.

The corn was loaded aboard the SS Alfonsin and SS Flamingo at

Coper, on the Adriatic coast of Yugoslavia, early in 1986. The ships were chartered by ITCO, a state-run Greek company, which paid £70 a ton for the corn. The ships then sailed to Salonika where ITCO, with the help of the Greek authorities, obtained fresh documents showing the corn to be Greek, not Yugoslav. The two vessels moved on to Antwerp, where the corn was sold at the European Community price of £150 a ton, a profit of £1.6 million for ITCO. Most of that money should have been paid into the EC's coffers as import duties.

The Greek swindle was rumbled, however, by someone in the trade, who tipped off the European Commission. A team of investigators was assembled from the commission's agriculture, customs and finance departments and sent to Greece. "We were obstructed at every turn," one told *The Times*. "Ministers even gave instructions to officials in the ports to lie to us."

Undeterred, the "detectives" crossed into Yugoslavia, where they found sufficient papers to prove the case. The Greek finance, economic and foreign ministers were informed and, when they failed to act or reprimand the culprits, the Greek authorities and ITCO were taken to the European Court of Justice. In September they were ordered to pay the full import duties, plus £600,000 in accumulated interest.

Source: *The Times*, 20 November 1989

Structural policy

Why is Community agriculture uncompetitive? History has bequeathed to Europe a very large number of farms, most being far too small to provide a reasonable income: small farms have high unit costs and produce little revenue. A farm can only expand to become a profitable business by increasing its land area, and as the supply of land is fixed it follows that an efficient agricultural industry means far fewer farms and *farmers*. Here is the problem: the Community has millions of farmers, most of whom would need to leave the land before agriculture could become efficient. Since the 1960s the Community has had measures for retraining farmers for other occupations or to help them to retire. But little money has been provided and this **structural policy** has had little impact. Enthusiasm for structural change was notably lacking in the early days of the EC when the economies of the Six were expanding rapidly. The widespread unemployment of more recent years has made any restructuring of farming far more difficult. Quite simply, there are no jobs for ex-farmers to go to; they might as well farm inefficiently as become unemployed.

Green currencies

The Community completed its price policy in 1968 – that is, agricultural prices throughout the Community had been gradually changed until they reached common levels. But then, events conspired to upset these common prices. A world system of fixed exchange rates had operated successfully for about 24 years, now it began to break up. The common prices for agricultural products were denominated in units of account (now **European Currency Units**) which translated into member states' currencies at fixed rates. In 1969 the French franc was devalued and the German mark revalued. At the new currency values, since agricultural prices were in units of account the prices of French agricultural products should have increased (there are now more francs per unit of account) whilst German prices should have fallen. Neither country was willing to permit these price changes, the French saying that higher food prices were inflationary and the Germans that lower prices would reduce farmers' incomes unacceptably. So although all other industries had to put up with the consequences of the currency changes the out-of-date currency values were retained in both countries just for agriculture; i.e. prices in France were lower and in Germany higher than the agreed common prices. To prevent these price differences distorting trade in agricultural products, a system of border taxes and subsidies was introduced. These **monetary compensatory amounts** (MCAs) became increasingly important as currency changes became more frequent within the Community. As they permitted the use of artificial exchange rates for internal agricultural trade, these rates became known as **green currencies**, an increasingly unfortunate use of the word in the 1990s now that 'green' is attached to fashionable environmental protection policies.

It is ironic that in a common market, the size of the MCAs became so large that real price differences for agricultural products often exceeded those existing between member states before the Community began. This is clearly a serious distortion of competition. Such price differences prevent the operation of comparative advantage, though even when it does work the results are so painful for the 'losing side' that some political intervention usually negates economic forces. The 1990 'lamb wars' will probably be settled with additional aid for the sufferers. MCAs are due to be abolished in the single market by the end of 1992. However no mechanism for their removal has yet been agreed.

Consequences of the CAP

Have the policy objectives been achieved? Certainly productivity has increased, and supplies assured, both partly the result of high prices. The manipulated price system has also stabilized prices. What is 'reasonable' cannot be objectively defined, so it is a matter of opinion whether or not prices to consumers are reasonable. What is beyond doubt is that the main objective of raising farm incomes has not been achieved, for farmers still have, on average, about half of the incomes of the non-farming members of society; their relative positions have not improved. Averages always hide much information. In the present case, consider who benefits from high prices – clearly the farmers who produce most. These large farmers also have low unit costs (economies of size). So the CAP is helping the larger, relatively wealthy farmers, whilst leaving the poorer small farmers still poor. As the policy transfers income from consumers to producers, it includes transfers from poor consumers – for even the poor must eat – to richer farmers! On equity grounds such income distribution effects have few supporters.

There are two other major areas affected by the CAP which must be considered: the financial and the economic consequences. The financial consequences arise from the need to dispose of the

Table 6 Budgetary expenditure of the EC, 1971–90 (million ECUs)

	Agricultural fund	Social fund	Regional fund	Industry energy research	Administration	Other	Totals	Agriculture percentage share
1971	1 884	57	–	65	132	152	2 289	82
1972	2 478	98	–	75	177	247	3 075	81
1973	3 769	269	–	69	239	294	4 641	81
1974	3 651	292	–	83	337	675	5 038	72
1975	4 587	360	150	99	375	643	6 214	74
1976	6 033	177	300	113	420	910	7 953	76
1977	6 464	325	373	163	497	883	8 705	74
1978	9 602	285	255	227	677	1 302	12 348	78
1979	10 736	596	672	288	864	1 448	14 603	74
1980	11 596	502	752	213	939	2 056	16 058	72
1981	11 446	547	2 264	218	1 035	3 025	18 546	62
1982	12 792	910	2 766	346	1 103	3 510	21 427	60
1983	16 331	801	2 266	1 216	1 162	2 990	24 766	66
1984	18 986	1 116	1 283	1 346	1 237	2 151	26 119	73
1985	20 546	1 413	1 624	707	1 333	2 600	28 223	73
1986	23 068	2 533	2 373	760	1 603	4 526	34 863	66
1987	23 939	2 542	2 562	965	1 740	3 721	35 469	67
1988†	27 532	2 299	3 093	1 204	1 947	6 187	42 261	65
1989*	29 683	2 950	3 920	1 363	2 150	4 773	44 838	66
1990*	30 205	3 322	4 705	1 788	2 401	4 389	46 808	65

Notes: †estimated, *forecast
Source: *European Economy*, vol. 42, 1989

surpluses which the high-price system generates. These financial costs are met by the **Agricultural Guarantee and Guidance Fund** (universally known by the acronym FEOGA from its title in French) which dominates the EC budget, accounting for about two-thirds of all budgetary expenditure on average as shown in Table 6. So large is this expenditure on agricultural support that little is left to finance other common policies. Consequently, the development of other common policies and the introduction of new ones is severely curtailed.

Economic efficiency

The economic consequences of the CAP are of two types – conventional and environmental. In terms of conventional economics, the fact that agriculture is much more heavily protected/subsidized than other industries means that it uses some resources which could be used more profitably elsewhere. Thus on the grounds of efficiency there is significant **resource misallocation** within the Community. As the other industrialized countries outside the EC have their own agricultural support systems, some even more protective than the CAP, the misallocation is of global significance. The protection of agriculture is believed to contribute to unemployment in EC manufacturing. It is argued that because the CAP expands EC agricultural production to the point of major dumping on world markets (EC is the world's second largest exporter of agricultural products) it must make countries which have a comparative advantage in agricultural production poorer. As a result their imports of manufactures from the EC are reduced, and it follows that so is employment in manufacturing industry. This problem is compounded by high food prices in the EC which help to raise costs via wages in other industries and damage their international competitiveness.

Green economics

Environmental economics are beyond the scope of this book, but some of the environmental side-effects of the CAP merit a mention in passing. The CAP has encouraged, through its high prices, the ploughing of chalk downs in the south of England, and moors in the north, which at world prices would have remained as grazing lands. Wild flowers, butterflies and many other insects, bird and mammal populations have all been much reduced. Putting a monetary value on environmental amenities is notoriously difficult – how would you value a beautiful view, or a colony of rare wild flowers? Public attention tends to concentrate on the damage caused by the

CAP, but it has its positive side too. Without the CAP's subsidization of livestock production in the remote and unprofitable regions of the EC – which account for huge areas of mountains, hills and moors etc. – agriculture would have disappeared from these regions. The loss of grazing animals would have resulted in the replacement of pleasant alpine meadows, for example, by unsightly bracken and scrub. Depopulation and a collapse of the infrastructure would have made tourism in such regions a thing of the past.

CAP reform

The failure of the CAP to provide 'fair' incomes for the small farmers despite its vast cost has led to the universal recognition that reform is necessary. Unfortunately the true economic costs are difficult to quantify and seem to make little impact on politicians; they therefore base their decisions almost entirely upon the financial costs although these are of secondary importance. So reforms are aimed at reducing the budgetary costs without addressing the other ill effects of the policy. The undesirable consequences of the CAP largely result from high prices, but reducing them significantly is regarded as politically unacceptable and politicians have sought other ways of reducing budgetary costs. In 1984 a **quota system** was introduced for milk. This limits the support for milk production to a predetermined quota output, with extra production attracting a much lower price. This reduces the surpluses which must be disposed of (as butter) and hence the costs. However, it still leaves the consumers paying high prices and supporting producers via an implicit food tax.

The quota principle was extended in 1988 to some of the major crops by a **stabilizer system**. This seeks to stabilize outputs and financial support costs by reducing the prices of outputs which exceed set thresholds (notice how words like 'stabilize' and 'threshold' are substituted for the politically less acceptable words 'limit' and 'quota' respectively). Although reform is the term used to describe the introduction of quotas and stabilizers it is clearly a gross exaggeration – since high prices with all their undesirable effects still apply to the vast bulk of output. Minor modification would be nearer the truth. *The Economist* has observed, bluntly, that, 'The EC has a grotesque agricultural policy'.

Targeting

What policy instruments would reduce economic and financial costs to much lower levels and achieve the objective of a more equitable distribution of incomes; i.e. higher incomes for small farmers? In a

Community whose economic philosophy is of the free market, artificially high prices for agriculture are anachronistic. Resources would be more efficiently allocated by a free market, but clearly this would not achieve higher incomes for farmers. However, in the absence of surpluses and their disposal costs finance would be freed to make direct income payments to farmers and to **target** payments on those in greatest need. This is an obvious economic solution, but since such overt transfer payments would be regarded as charity by farmers, there are substantial political difficulties in adopting such a radical reform.

Conclusion

The Community has been remarkably reluctant to undertake any significant reform of the CAP. However, the importance of trade to the Community may turn out to be the lever which forces reform. As discussed in the previous chapter, the success of the Uruguay round of trade negotiations depends to a large extent upon the EC agreeing to liberalize agricultural trade. In late autumn 1990 the Community and the USA appear to have reached stalemate over this issue. After eight protracted meetings of the Council of Agricultural Ministers the EC reached an internal agreement to offer to reduce its subsidies to agriculture by 30 per cent over a period of ten years from 1986 (15 per cent had happened anyway by 1990), with compensatory income payments to farmers which are yet to be decided. This minimal offer, achieved with great difficulty in the Community, compares with a minimum reduction of 70 per cent demanded by the rest of the GATT countries!

KEY WORDS

Price elasticities	Monetary compensatory
Economic efficiency	amounts
Target Price	Green currencies
Variable import levy	Agricultural Guarantee and
Implicit food tax	Guidance Fund
Intervention system	Resource misallocation
Structural policy	Quota system
European Currency Units	Stabilizer system
	Target

Reading list

Cook, M. and Healey, N., *Current Topics in International Economics*, Anforme, 1990.

Hill, B.E., *The Common Agricultural Policy, Past, Present and Future*, Methuen, 1984.

Hill, B.E., *Agriculture*, Open University, 1988.

Paisley, R. and Quillfeldt, J., *Economics Investigated*, chap. 6, Collins, 1989.

Essay topics

1. Assess the advantages and disadvantages for the United Kingdom of the Common Agricultural Policy of the European Community. (University of Oxford Delegacy of Local Examinations, 1986).

2. Distinguish between consumers' surplus, producers' surplus and economic rent. Discuss the effect on each of these if the government introduces a guaranteed minimum price for wheat above the free market equilibrium price. (University of Oxford Delegacy of Local Examinations, 1990)

3. Compare and contrast the effects on price and output of: subsidies on food to consumers; subsidies to producers of food; controlled minimum prices for food. (University of Oxford Delegacy of Local Examinations, 1988)

4. Using supply and demand analysis, examine the problems generally faced by agricultural producers. Assess the likely consequences of government attempts to remedy these problems. (University of London School Examinations Board, 1989)

5. Why and how do governments intervene to regulate the prices of agricultural commodities? (University of London School Examinations Board, 1986)

6. 'Agriculture is often said to resemble the economist's model of perfect competition, yet governments frequently intervene to determine agricultural output or prices.' Explain this statement and compare two methods of intervention. (Associated Examining Board, 1988)

7. Explain what is meant by dumping in the context of international trade. Discuss whether or not dumping can or should be prevented. (Associated Examining Board, 1987)

8. 'Agricultural protection is the bane of the EEC.' Discuss this comment on the Common Agricultural Policy. (Oxford and Cambridge Schools Examination Board, 1989)

Data Response Question 3

This task is based on a Welsh Joint Examinations Commitee question in 1988. Below is an extract from an article on the World Bank Development Report 1986, published in *The Times* on 8 July 1986. Study the passage and then answer the following questions.

1. Explain what is meant in the article by 'artificially high prices'.
2. Explain with the use of a diagram why milk surpluses increased during the 1970s.
3. Why do both consumers *and* taxpayers share the cost of the Common Agricultural Policy?
4. Why might a system of quotas reduce the milk surpluses and government spending, but not benefit consumers?
5. Why is it argued that the Common Agricultural Policy harms developing countries?
6. Why does most of the benefit 'end up in higher land prices in the long run'?

The World Bank has launched a devastating attack on the Common Agricultural Policy and its equivalents, estimating that farming support and protection is costing taxpayers and consumers in the industrial countries of the OECD more than $100 billion. But the Bank's study concludes that only about half this cost benefits producers. Most of the benefit ends up in higher land prices or rents rather than helping farmers' incomes in the long run.

Regimes such as the EEC's Common Agricultural Policy have raised output uneconomically at home by intervention to maintain artificially high prices. The CAP also imposes protection against imports and subsidises exports. This combination has a substantial adverse effect on the developing countries where agriculture often accounts for 35%–40% of gross domestic product and is vital for economic growth.

During the 1970s improvements in milk yields reduced dairy costs while official milk support prices were actually raised. Governments found themselves flooded with milk surpluses and government spending soared, increasing sixfold in the EEC. Instead of lowering prices and letting consumers benefit from the technical progress however, governments have attempted to remedy this situation by the introduction of production quotas.

Chapter Five

Other common policies

After agricultural support expenditures have come close to exhausting the budget there is little left for any other policies. Nevertheless, regional, social and fisheries policies exist.

The Treaty of Rome does not explicitly call for a **regional policy,** but it contains numerous references to the need for balanced regional development. Article 3 includes amongst the Community activities the establishment of a **European Investment Bank** (EIB) which, as discussed below, has played a major role in regional developments. The same article requires 'the creation of a European Social Fund in order to improve the possibilities of employment for workers and to contribute to the raising of their standard of living'. The Community concentrates on economic aspects of social policies, such as employment, sexual discrimination and working conditions, leaving other aspects of social policy – housing, health, social welfare payments and education – to national governments. The Treaty of Rome did not explicitly call for a common fisheries policy, though Article 38 mentions fish and fish products and treats fish as though it was part of agriculture – the Article 39 objectives for which are deemed to apply (see the previous chapter). The fisheries policy was developed in the early seventies – the principles being laid down rather conveniently just before applicants with very significant fishing interests joined.

The need for a common regional policy
When the Community began, its members already had their own disparate regional policies. Consider the problem of a relatively poor 'backward' region which a national government wishes to assist. The provision of special subsidies may be the desired policy instrument, but at what level do such subsidies cease merely to compensate for regional disadvantages and become unfair national aids which distort Community competition? Clearly it is essential to have some community-level policy coordination if competitive forces are not to be negated.

A major reason for national regional policies is the long-term decline of traditional industries such as textiles, coal, steel and shipbuilding. These have been the main economic activities in much of the north of England, for example, and their decline has contributed greatly to unemployment in that region. (As noted earlier, the ECSC has been much involved in aiding adjustment in the coal and steel industries.)

The operation of the European Community itself provides further reasons for developing regional policies. In the short term, changes in trading patterns following the formation of the EC could be expected to lead to regional adjustment problems. In the longer term the positive economic benefits of applying the law of comparative advantage, and of economies of size, have their negative side: in each country some activities will prosper, but others will be uncompetitive and *must* be allowed to fail. Unfortunately successful enterprises are often distant from those which fail, making the transfer of resources slow and difficult. So new regional problems are constantly created.

The European Investment Bank has concentrated its activities on financing improvements to infrastructure (roads, water and energy supplies etc.) and investments in enterprises. As a bank it is making loans and charging interest so that its influence in any one region owes more to national and local initiatives than to positive central policies. Nevertheless its financing has been heavily concentrated in the poorer regions of the poorer countries. Originally the Bank's activities were confined to internal Community loans, but later were extended to other countries. In the 1980s about 10 per cent of the Bank's funds have been loaned externally. Most of its resources are raised by borrowing on the international capital market.

In 1975 the Community expanded its regional activities by establishing a **European Regional Development Fund** (ERDF). This is funded by the Community budget and is able to provide more traditional forms of regional development finance than can the EIB – capital grants, input subsidies etc. Its main expenditures are for special projects and programmes in the poorer areas of the Community. ERDF contributes 50–55 per cent of the cost of these activities, the remainder coming from national sources. Consequently the Community policy is more of a supplement to national regional policies than a fully developed common policy. As budgetary funds are limited, particularly by the fact that most are destined for the CAP, further developments seem unlikely in the near future (see budgetary expenditures in Table 6).

Social policy

Initially the policy was mainly concerned with the free movement of labour, one of the essential attributes of the common market. Mass unemployment and concern over disadvantaged groups of workers has gradually changed the emphasis. The **European Social Fund** (ESF), like the ERDF, contributes 50–55 per cent to certain national expenditures. One of its major focusses is unemployment, and expenditure has been concentrated on vocational training, retraining, job creation and assisting women who wish to return to work. Like the ERDF it is largely supplemental to national activities and its scope is severely limited by a lack of budgetary funds (see budgetary expenditures in Table 6).

Working conditions are a second major focus of attention. The Community has a different attitude from that of the Conservative UK government of recent years. It emphasizes the rights of workers to unite, negotiate and participate in industry, and wishes to encourage such collective activities. In contrast the UK has concentrated on the rights of workers as individuals and has tended to weaken collective rights. Not surprisingly the recent development of the EC's Social Charter has not been welcomed in all quarters of the UK.

The Social Charter

The Commission felt that the introduction of the single market, with its stimulation of business, should be balanced by the development of social conditions which would ensure that all citizens would benefit. The economic programme was to be given a `human face'. Accordingly, the **Social Charter** was produced, its first draft appearing in May 1989. It was discussed in June by the Economic and Social Affairs Committee followed by the European Council. It was broadly welcomed by eleven member states but opposed by the UK. The Council made the following three points:

- In the construction of the single market, social aspects should be accorded the same importance as economic aspects.
- In the creation of the single market, job creation was to be given top priority.
- Implementation should comply with the principle of **'subsidiarity'**.

The latter term requires some explanation: subsidiarity means that action should only be taken at Community level when this offers a better way of achieving an objective than leaving it to member states. The UK seized upon this term and took it to heart, claiming that the whole topic was best dealt with by members states.

55

The Charter covers twelve categories of fundamental social rights:

(a) Freedom of movement of workers within the Community
(b) 'Fair' remuneration, protection to part-time workers
(c) Improved working conditions, including minimum annual paid leave and a weekly break from work
(d) Workers and unemployed to receive adequate social protection and social security payments
(e) Freedom of association and collective bargaining, including the right to choose whether or not to belong to a trade union and the right to strike
(f) Workers should be able to train and retrain throughout their working lives
(g) Equal treatment for men and women
(h) Workers should have rights relating to information, consultation and participation, particularly at times of restructuring, redundancies or the introduction of new technology
(i) Health and safety at work
(j) Protection of children and young people: this involves a minimum employment age, maximum hours of work, entitlement to vocational training after compulsory education
(k) Decent standard of living on retirement
(l) All disabled people should have additional help towards social and professional integration.

Not all of these 'fundamental rights' exist in the UK. For example, under (c) there is no statutory right to annual paid leave in the UK, although this right already exists in all other members except Italy. Similarly, only the UK and Denmark do not impose a limit on working hours (as publicity given to the hours worked by junior hospital doctors may remind us). Under (e) there is no statutory right to strike in the UK, instead there is only a limited system of trade union immunities. Under (h), only in the UK, Ireland and Greece are there no works councils which must be informed of major developments.

The Social Charter was much discussed during the summer of 1989. It introduced a new term 'subsidiarity', discussed earlier, and greatly approved of by the UK government. Indeed the UK argued throughout that most of the Charter's concerns would be better left in the hands of national governments. By the end of the year the Charter had been accepted by eleven nations, isolating the UK in opposition. As a result, proposed measures to implement the Charter are very limited in scope, being restricted to matters such as the treatment of immigrant workers, which are clearly of community-level interest. The development of a comprehensive common social policy seems a long way off. In the meantime there are many confusions. Some are specific – such as the retirement age in the UK, which used to be 60 for women and 65 for men, although under existing UK law sexual discrimination is illegal, and the UK has vaguely agreed to introduce a new retirement age 'sometime'. At the general level the question is what happens next? There is nothing to stop the eleven proposing social measures in accordance with the Charter. If the UK did not wish to be outvoted and so have such measures forced upon her, she would have to claim special national interests and try to invoke the power of veto – and then be accused by the rest of the Community of being 'non-European'. These issues have become very sensitive, as the box giving the opinion of a House of Lords Select Committee explains.

Opinion of the House of Lords Select Committee on the EC

30. The most striking feature of the negotiations on the proposed Community Social Charter is the extent to which the Charter has become a symbolic issue. It is symbolic first of the Community's determination to avoid being seen as a purely commercial institution, whose work is remote from the concerns of ordinary citizens. But it has also become, along with full United Kingdom membership of the European Monetary System, a touchstone for judging the United Kingdom's commitment to the development of the Community. They consider that this is regrettable, but believe that it must now be accepted as fact. The Committee recently argued in the context of proposals for economic and monetary union that the current debate on the future of the Community, and of Europe as a whole, makes it essential that the United Kingdom should persuade its Community partners of its European credentials. The Social Charter also raises sensitive issues about the balance between national and Community powers, and about the future direction of the Community. It is of great importance that the United Kingdom should not appear to turn its back on Europe, so that it can play its full part in negotiations.

31. It is clear that there is a groundswell of support in other Member States for some form of Social Charter. Calls for reassurances that the Single Market programme will benefit workers, children and old people, as well as shareholders and managers, are perfectly understandable, as is the opinion that the time has come to draw together and to highlight the various social provisions in the Treaty of Rome. There is no reason why a statement of the social benefits of the Single Market should imply a mandate for unrealistic regulation which could smother economic growth. A social dimension to the Community will have to fall into step behind wealth and job creation, and the grant of rights does imply corresponding obligations. But the Charter's Preamble already makes this clear by stressing that employment development and creation must be given absolute priority and that the Community must respond to the competitive challenges of the future.

Source: HL paper 6–I, Session 1989/90, 3 September.

It is likely that the Commission will bring forward some social issues as proposed regulations or directives before the end of 1992 – the intended date for the completion of the single market. The response of the UK is unpredictable if, as seems probable, this coincides with the run-up to a British general election.

Fisheries policy

A fisheries policy was agreed by the Six in 1970 to come into force in 1971. At the time there were four applicants for EC membership: Denmark, Ireland, Norway and the UK, all with major fishing interests, and with no say in the new policy. Many suspected that the timing of the new policy agreement was to ensure the adoption of a policy which would favour the Six in an enlarged Community. Indeed, the predetermined fisheries policy was a major factor in Norway's decision not to accept membership at the conclusion of accession negotiations (an estimated 20 per cent of the Norwegian population relied on fishing for a living – as fishermen, shipbuilders, fish processors, and providers of a wide range of services to this industry). The other three countries managed to obtain temporary concessions, which would last for ten years.

The policy adopted was for free access for all Community fishermen to all Community waters, with a common internal market for fish. Such a policy is economic nonsense – it made no provision for the conservation of fish stocks, indeed, it encouraged the attitude that 'if we don't catch the fish someone else will'. The UK and other new members disliked the policy because it opened up the UK coastal waters, traditionally the exclusive preserve of national fishermen, to all Community fishermen. Temporary concessions negotiated by the three new members permitted them to retain exclusive fishing rights in coastal waters for ten years before the Community 'free-for-all' fisheries policy affected them. However, they had either to attempt to change the fisheries policy during those ten years or face the fact that they would have to give up exclusive rights to many of Europe's best fisheries for nothing in return.

In 1975 Iceland declared a 200 mile exclusive fishing zone, precipitating a 'cod war' with the UK, which had a large distant deep-sea fishing fleet dependent on fishing this Icelandic area. Exclusive fishing zones had mostly been between 3 and 12 miles and international attention now turned to much wider zones. A United Nations International Conference on the Law of the Sea deliberated the problem between 1974 and 1976 without defining a new law. However, after the conference Norway, Canada and the USA announced 200 mile exclusion zones, and the Community, under great pressure from the UK which threatened unilateral action, did likewise.

There was now a clear need to rethink the common fisheries policy. It had to deal not merely with coastal waters forming exclusion zones up to 12 miles, but a huge area which included much of the North Sea. There were two main problems: first, to decide on access of Community fishermen to the enlarged 'Community pond'; second, the 200 mile exclusion zone would exclude fishermen of third countries who had traditionally fished some of this area. At first the UK demanded extended exclusion zones of 100 miles for her own fleets, claiming that such a wide zone was necessary to compensate for the loss of access to other fisheries such as the Icelandic ones. Eventually attention turned away from exclusion zones to the allocation of the 'total available catch'. The latter is a conservation concept and refers to the maximum catch which can be sustained in the long term without the running down of the fish stocks.

A new policy agreement was finally reached in 1983. For each major fish species it allocated the total available catch, and introduced other conservation measures such as minimum mesh sizes for nets. The UK share of the catch was set reasonably generously at almost 30 per cent. Some third countries were also allocated shares of the Community catch with the Commission negotiating reciprocal arrangements for Community fleets to fish their waters. The new policy included some measures to assist with the restructuring and modernization of the fishing industry, and of course, a common market in fish and fish products. Expenditures on the fisheries policy have been very modest – 281 mECU in 1988, less than one-hundredth of agricultural expenditures.

KEY WORDS

Regional policy
European Investment Bank
European Regional
  Development Fund

European Social Fund
Social Charter
Subsidiarity

Reading list

Swann, D., *The Economics of the Common Market*, Penguin Books, 1988.

Armstrong, H. and Taylor, J., *Regional Economics*, chap. 6, Heinemann Educational, 1990.

Essay topics

1. Critically examine the economic reasons for having common regional and social policies.
2. Outline the original fisheries policy and explain why it was reformed in 1983. Given that the objectives are identical to those for agriculture, why has the fisheries policy attracted relatively little support expenditure.
3. Write on three of the following aspects of the EEC:
   (a) The entry of Spain and Portugal
   (b) The Common Fisheries Policy
   (c) Trade relations between EEC and USA
   (d) The European Social Fund.
   (Oxford and Cambridge Schools Examination Board, 1986)

Data Response Question 4

This task is based on an Associated Examining Board question in 1989. Read the article on 'Two nations' which is taken from *Lloyds Bank Economic Bulletin*, May 1987, and then answer the following questions.

1. To what extent does the data confirm the common assertion that there is a North–South divide?
2. Explain why economic theory might suggest that 'a regional bias in terms of income and employment would generate the migration of workers towards the more prosperous areas'.
3. Critically assess the statement that 'Migration to areas of higher employment would eventually even out regional unemployment rates'.
4. Why may the existence of large regional disparities mean that a 'considerable reduction in unemployment would not be achieved by a general expansion of demand'.

Two nations?

The "North–South divide" is becoming a popular theme for discussion among commentators on the UK economic scene. A common assertion is that, by drawing a line from the river Severn to the Wash, the country can be split into two quite distinct areas, with enormously different economic performances. North of the line lies a depressed region, with run-down industries, urban decay, mass unemployment and little hope for the future. South of the line lies a prosperous economy, showing rapid industrial expansion into high technology and a booming service sector.

The map shows 1985 gross domestic product per head in the different regions of the UK. However GDP is only one measure of disparities in regional performance. The table presents some other indicators.

GDP PER HEAD BY REGION, 1985

SCOTLAND
97.3

NORTHERN
IRELAND
74.8

NORTH
92.9

YORKSHIRE &
HUMBERSIDE
91.8

N.
WEST
96.0

EAST
MIDLANDS
95.7

EAST
ANGLIA
100.8

WEST
MIDLANDS
92.3

WALES
88.8

SOUTH
EAST
114.8

SOUTH WEST
93.8

The numbers show regional GDP per head as a percentage of the national average. Regions with above average GDP per head are shaded.

Effects of regional inequality

Economic theory would suggest that a regional bias in terms of income and employment would generate the migration of workers

	Personal disposable income per head, 1985	Unemployment (% of working population Jan. 1987)	Long-term unemployed (% of unemployed Jan. 1987)	Net migration with the rest of UK (thousands) 1985
South East	4725	8.5	36.2	-16
East Anglia	4244	9.3	33.5	+19
Scotland	4181	15.1	39.2	-8
South West	4152	10.4	32.7	+41
North West	4074	14.3	44.3	-16
E. Midlands	4066	11.4	39.2	+6
W. Midlands	3997	13.8	46.3	-9
Yorks and Humb.	3923	13.8	42.0	-12
North	3919	16.9	44.3	-9
Wales	3778	14.3	40.6	+5
N. Ireland	3538	19.3	50.0	-3

towards the more prosperous areas. But the evidence suggests that net regional migration is very low. Migration within areas tends to be larger than net migration between areas. The figures also show a net outward migration from the South-East. There are several factors which may prevent people moving to the more prosperous areas. Migration is costly, the incentive to move may be low if similar jobs in other regions pay a similar wage, and even if there is a significant difference in expected income between regions, this may be insufficient to compensate for regional disparities in the cost of living.

Migration to areas of higher employment would eventually even out regional unemployment rates, but at present rates it would take many years to achieve this. The alternative is the migration of employers to areas of high unemployment. Upward pressure on pay in the prosperous areas, together with widening office cost disparities, are encouraging employers to move staff out to lower cost regions.

Large regional disparities also have important implications for government policy. They suggest that a considerable reduction in unemployment would not be achieved by a general expansion of demand. Instead a more active regional policy is required, including measures to increase labour mobility.

Chapter Six

Economic and monetary union

'London is the capital of Paris, and Paris is the capital of Rome, and Rome . . . . no, that's all wrong, I'm certain!' (said Alice)

Economic and monetary union is the final stage in economic integration. It means the replacement of national currencies with a single European currency and centralized control of monetary and economic policies. It involves such a pooling of sovereignty that political union is the only logical conclusion.

The EMU debate

There is a limit to the degree of market integration which can be achieved so long as national currencies and economic policies exist. Even in the absence of tariff barriers, and if all technical standards and company law were harmonized and all non-tariff barriers removed, national currencies would still inhibit competition. They do this in two ways. First, the conversion of one currency into another adds to costs. Second, the possibility that the exchange rates between currencies may change during a deal adds substantially to uncertainty. These uncertainties are magnified by differences in inflation rates. Finally, different economic policies in member states result in different rates of interest and different methods and rates of taxation both for companies and consumers. It follows that the full benefits of the internal market can only be achieved by full economic and monetary union.

Brief mention should be made here of the CAP. One of its problems has been that of **uncommon prices** caused by the 'green' currency exchange rate system. A common currency would resolve this difficulty and ease the operation of the CAP.

What is the economic case against EMU?

Take the case of a member country with balance of payments problems causing its exchange rate to fall. It has three policy options: using its reserves of gold and foreign currency to support its desired exchange rate, raising its interest rate to increase the international demand for its currency, or finally, curing the underlying problem. For example, it may be that a high inflation rate is making the country uncompetitive and anti-inflationary policies are required. Any or all of these policies may fail and then equilibrium must be restored by altering the exchange rate, or permitting it to be determined by market forces. If the country in question is locked into an EMU, it possesses none of these options – its currency is the common currency, fixed in terms of its partners – it has the same rate of inflation as its partners. So if its workers demand higher wages and fail to increase productivity accordingly they will become unemployed; national economic policy has no power beyond that of persuasion to help them.

In reality these arguments against EMU are political in that control over economic policy instruments is lost by individual countries. This loss of control is indeed very substantial. The possibility of a major recession in one country or region implies corrective action involving considerable resource transfers; ultimately regional policies as part of a central budget and central economic policy control would be necessary.

As the EMU debate turns out to be largely political the present discussion must avoid taking sides and will concentrate on the economic issues. These deal with how EMU may be achieved, and chart developments in the Community.

How can EMU be achieved?

There are four essential elements to EMU. First is the introduction of a **single currency**. This implies two further elements, the need for a central bank, and a central budget and economic policy. In turn these require the development of political control. A single currency, the first hurdle, is the one which appears to attract most attention –not surprisingly, for once agreed to the other elements of EMU must follow.

A single currency could be achieved at a stroke by agreeing that from some particular date exchange rates would be fixed. National currencies would then gradually be replaced by the new EC currency. Alternatively, the permitted variation in exchange rates between members would be reduced until they became zero – the fixed exchange rate stage would be achieved gradually. A third possibility is the parallel circulation of national currencies and an EC currency, the former being eventually replaced by the latter. The practical problems of having a common currency in parallel with national currencies whose exchange rates are not fixed make this unlikely to be adopted as the chosen Community pathway. Perhaps this is why the parallel currency option was proposed by Mrs Thatcher's government, which was strongly opposed to EMU.

A gradual approach to a single currency was attempted by the Community with its 'snake in the tunnel' introduced in 1972. Members' currencies were permitted to vary against each other within a 2.25 per cent band (the snake) but by 4.5 per cent against other currencies (the tunnel). The scheme was introduced by the original six members but was also joined by the four applicant countries – Denmark, Norway, Ireland and the UK (the latter two still had a common currency). However, the international system of exchange rates came under heavy pressure, and in 1973 there was a worldwide shift from fixed to floating exchange rates. In 1972 the UK allowed the pound to float out of the snake and tunnel, followed by Ireland and Denmark though the Danes rejoined. In 1973 Italy floated out, followed by France in 1974 which rejoined in 1975 only to leave again in 1976. By 1977 only half the Community remained in the snake. This move towards EMU had failed but there were some positive gains. Firstly, from the beginning it had been agreed that the Council of Ministers should meet three times a year to lay down guidelines for short-term economic management in member states and this means of economic cooperation was retained. Secondly, in 1973, in recognition of the need to develop regional policy the European Regional Development Fund had been inaugurated. Finally, also in 1973, the **European Monetary Cooperation Fund** (EMCF) was established to manage the 'snake in the tunnel', and this survived to become important later in connection with the **European Monetary System**.

The European Monetary System

The EMS was introduced in 1979 with two main aims: first to increase economic convergence, and second to create a zone of monetary stability within the Community to foster internal trade. Of course these aims have to be seen against the long-term aim of EMU to which they would contribute.

As part of the EMS each member state (including the UK) handed 20 per cent of its gold and foreign currency reserves to EMCF in return for ECUs (discussed below). These can be used in transactions within the Community. The ECU (**European Currency Unit**) was introduced (replacing the very similar European Unit of Account) as a composite currency; i.e. it is a unit based on a 'weighted basket' of members' currencies. The weight assigned to each currency is in proportion to the relative size of that country's economy. As Germany is the largest economy in the Community it has a large weight in the ECU, so if the deutschmark increases in value it noticeably increases the value of the ECU. The present composition of the ECU is shown in Table 7.

Table 7 Composition of the ECU from 21 September 1989

Currency	Weighting coefficient (%)	Amount in National currency
Belgian franc	7.6	3.301
Danish Krone	2.45	0.1976
German mark	30.1	0.6242
Greek drachma	0.8	1.440
Portugese escuda	0.8	1.393
French franc	19.0	1.332
Dutch florin	9.4	0.2198
Irish punt	1.1	0.008552
Luxembourg franc	0.3	0.130
Italian lira	10.15	151.8
Spanish peseta	5.3	6.885
British pound	13.0	0.08784
Totals	100.0	1.0 ECU

Sources: *Bulletin EC*, 6–1989 and 9–1989

The **Exchange Rate Mechanism** (ERM) is the central part of the EMS and its operation is intended to provide the zone of monetary stability. The currency of each member has a specific value (parity) in terms of the ECU. In turn this means that each currency has a parity value in terms of each of the other member currencies. Any one currency is permitted to vary by plus or minus 2.25 per cent against any other member currency. When this margin is reached the two central banks concerned must intervene to keep within the limits. There is a second element to the mechanism, a **divergence indicator.** This is three-quarters of a country's permitted variation against the ECU. When this indicator is reached the country is expected to take corrective action. Thus if the currency falls in value the government might increase interest rates, increase taxation or support the currency.

The simplified version of a currency's permitted variation against the ECU is in practice complicated by that currency's inclusion in the value of the ECU. This is most obvious for the deutschmark because of its 30 per cent weight in the ECU. The permitted variation is ±2.25 (1 – weight) per cent; so the divergence indicator for the deutschmark, three-quarters of this, is only 1.18 per cent. In contrast the Irish punt is only 1.1 per cent of the ECU so its divergence indicator is virtually three-quarters of 2.25, i.e. 1.7 per cent. For the Spanish peseta the limit to variation is 6 per cent rather than 2.25 per cent, but the Italian lira has recently moved from this wide band to the 2.25 band.

The UK persistently refused to join the ERM, but under political pressure from other members agreed to join 'when the time is right'. The Chancellor decided that this time had come in the middle of October 1990. Initially the UK pound is a wide-band currency having a 6 per cent variation limit. Greece and Portugal have not yet joined.

Table 8, extracted from the *Financial Times* of 12 September 1990, shows how several of the currencies stood in relation to the ECU *at that date.*

Table 8 EMS European currency unit rates

	ECU central rates	Currency amounts against ECU 11 Sept.	Change from central rate (%)	Divergence limit (%)
Belgian franc	42.1679	42.3430	+0.42	±1.5508
Danish krone	7.79845	7.87127	+0.93	±1.6453
German mark	2.04446	2.05962	+0.74	±1.1762
French franc	6.85684	6.90094	+0.64	±1.3618
Dutch guilder	2.30358	2.32143	+0.77	±1.5272
Irish punt	0.763159	0.767355	+0.55	±1.6689
Italian lira	1529.70	1536.11	+0.42	±1.5162
Spanish peseta	132.889	129.227	-2.76	±4.2705

Changes are for ECU: therefore positive change denotes a weak currency

Source: *Financial Times*, 12 September 1990

Appraisal of the EMS

The objectives of the EMS are economic convergence and stability, important prerequisites for economic and monetary union. **Real convergence** is the convergence of EC economies to the highest current EC living standards through the catching up of the poorer countries and regions. The EMS cannot directly cause this convergence but it can help to produce the stable economic environment in which real convergence can occur. **Nominal convergence** implies convergence towards the lowest rates of inflation, and to balance-of-payments and budget balances which together encourage more stable exchange rates – the ideal for EMU is exchange rates which are so stable that they can be fixed, and so be replaced with a single currency.

There are two indicators of nominal convergence, the rate of inflation itself, and the changes in labour costs which are a major factor causing inflation. These two indicators are shown in Tables 9 and 10. They show that inflation rates and changes in labour costs are much lower in the seven member states in the narrow-band ERM than in other Community countries. Italy and Spain appear to be converging towards these seven. The UK compares very poorly with the seven on both indicators.

So long as inflation rates differ between member states there will be strains in the EMS. Accordingly there have been various alterations in exchange rates, with, generally, the countries with the higher inflation rates devaluing and those with lower rates revaluing. This has provided an incentive for countries to keep inflation low, or become less competitive than fellow members. Another significant strain in the EMS is the difference in relative attractiveness of member currencies. Whenever there is pressure on the American dollar speculative funds flood into the deutschmark, and this has been a factor in some exchange rate **realignments**. The ERM was

Table 9 The rate of inflation in the Community, 1980 and 1985–90

	1980	1985	1986	1987	1988	1989	1990*
Greece	21.6	18.3	22.0	15.6	14.0	14.4	20.5
Portugal	21.4	19.4	13.8	10.0	10.0	12.8	13.2
United Kingdom	16.2	5.3	4.4	3.9	5.0	6.1	7.0
Wide-band ERM countries							
Italy	20.2	9.0	5.7	5.0	4.8	6.0	6.1
Spain	16.5	8.2	8.7	5.4	5.1	6.6	6.8
Narrow-band ERM countries							
Maximum	18.6	5.8	3.4	4.1	4.9	4.7	4.0
Average	9.0	3.8	1.1	1.7	1.8	3.2	2.8

Inflation is measured as the annual percentage change in the private consumption deflator.
* Forecast.

Source: *European Economy*, vol. 42, 1989; and vol. 46, 1990

Table 10 Unit labour costs in the Community, 1980 and 1985–90

	1980	1985	1986	1987	1988	1989	1990*
		Annual percentage change					
Greece	15.6	20.8	12.2	12.0	15.1	18.6	14.4
Portugal	19.5	19.1	12.2	11.4	9.2	8.9	8.8
United Kingdom	21.7	4.7	4.5	5.0	6.4	7.9	7.2
Wide-band ERM countries							
Italy	18.9	8.1	5.4	5.9	6.1	6.4	5.4
Spain	12.3	5.6	8.5	6.2	4.3	6.4	5.7
Narrow-band ERM countries							
Maximum	18.6	4.5	5.6	10.6	3.7	2.3	3.2
Minimum	5.0	0.4	1.7	-0.8	-0.4	-0.9	1.3
Average	9.2	2.8	2.4	1.8	0.5	1.2	1.7

* Forecast.

Source: *European Economy,* vol. 42, 1989

not designed to cope with such third-country pressures and some further mechanism seems desirable. The ERM also significantly constrains any one member country's economic policy options. If the French, for example, wished to reflate by increasing demand, much of the effect would be transmitted to other member states, and the French balance of payments would suffer and the franc begin to fall. The permitted margins to the franc's fall would soon be reached and France would be expected to maintain its ECU parity by reversing its reflationary policy. Clearly, economic policy decisions need to be taken in common if they are to work. Because the ECU is dominated by the deutschmark the other ERM countries are necessarily strongly influenced by German economic policy. This effect may become even more marked in future following German reunification.

It is widely accepted that the ERM has assisted nominal convergence, but much more policy convergence is necessary before real convergence can occur, and this means giving up more national sovereignty. Most members are reluctant to do this, and the UK is strongly opposed. Yet the Single European Act, agreed by all members, explicitly calls for new measures to ensure the coordination of economic and monetary policies!

At the summit of heads of government in Dublin in the spring of 1990 it was agreed that work on economic and monetary union should proceed at an inter–governmental conference to take place in Rome in December. The Dublin communique said that this should 'conclude its work rapidly with the objective of ratification by member states before the end of 1992'. In line with the Dublin decisions the Commission published in August 1990 its proposals for the second stage of EMU to begin on 1 January 1993, and to be of short duration. The major element of the Commission's paper for the second stage is the proposed setting up of a system of European central banks which it calls '**Eurofed**'. This would be subject to three fundamental principles: its primary objective should be price stability; it would be independent from national governments and Community authorities; and finally it should be democratically accountable. Its president should be appointed by the European Council following consultation with the European Parliament. Stage three would consist of the introduction of the ECU as the single currency, when this had been agreed by the European Council.

Conclusion

These topics clearly raise both political and economic issues which must be kept apart in the mind of the economist. On the economic benefits of EMU an empirical study, *One Market, One Money*, published in November 1990 by the Commission (with the support and advice of several economists outside the Commission) produces some interesting conclusions. Inflation will be reduced, exchange rate transactions costs will be removed, both contributing to a significant reduction in uncertainty and so encouraging an expansion in investment. The forecast increase in Community GDP resulting from EMU is of the order of 6 per cent and is dynamic in nature – that is approximately equal to the economic benefits of the Single Market which were detailed in Chapter 2. These findings underline the strength of the economic case for EMU.

KEY WORDS

Uncommon prices	Exchange Rate Mechanism
Single currency	Divergence indicator
Snake in the tunnel	Real convergence
European Monetary	Nominal convergence
Cooperation Fund	Realignments
European Monetary System	Eurofed
European Currency Unit	

Reading list

Cook, M. and Healey, N., *Current Topics in International Economics*, chap. 2, Anforme, 1990.

Cook, M. and Healey, N., *Current Topics in Applied Economics*, chap. 7, Anforme, 1990.

'ERM: Better late than never', *Lloyds Bank Bulletin*, November 1990.

McDonald, F., 'Monetary Union and Sovereignty in UK policy making', *British Economic Survey*, Autumn 1990.

Wickens, M., European monetary union, pros & cons, *Economic Review*, May 1990.

Essay topics

1. Look at Tables 9 and 10 and consider if there is any relationship between inflation and labour costs. If there is a relationship is it affected by ERM membership?
2. Describe the main features of the European Monetary System. Assess the arguments for and against UK membership of the system. (Associated Examining Board, 1987)
3. 'The time is ripe for Britain to join the EMS.' Comment. (Oxford and Cambridge Schools Examination Board, 1988)

Data Response Question 5

The ERM

Read the description of the Exchange Rate Mechanism of the European Monetary System, written in early 1991, and answer the following questions.

1. The terms 'Exchange Rate Mechanism' and 'European Monetary System' should not be confused with each other. Explain why.
2. Why does the burden of adjustment tend to fall upon deficit countries under exchange rate systems like the ERM?
3. Explain how and why the 'anti-inflationary' tendency of the ERM is likely to be seen as desirable, at the same time as its 'deflationary' bias might be regarded as being undesirable.
4. What are the consequences for the monetary and budgetary policies of individual states of a movement towards a common currency and central bank?

The Exchange Rate Mechanism (ERM) is, in effect, a system of pegged exchange rates, with a certain amount of movement allowed either side of parity. Under such arrangements, dating back to Bretton Woods, the burden has always been upon deficit countries to make adjustments, with less of the onus on surplus countries.

An important difference between the ERM and previous pegged rates is that currencies such as the pound and franc are effectively tied to the deutschmark, which is the strongest currency. Thus countries like the UK and France have to try to bring their inflation levels closely in line with that of Germany in order to remain competitive, and since devaluation is not an option (another important difference) they have to do this by restricting demand. The ERM is therefore both *anti-inflationary* and *deflationary*.

The UK has chosen to deflate through a policy of high interest rates. Consumer spending has proved to be relatively inelastic with respect to interest rates, but the recession of 1990-91 shows that they have eventually had an impact. However, high interest rates have also had unpleasant side effects. Investment has been reduced at a time of low growth, and unemployment. Some commentators have suggested that the pound entered the ERM at too high a level, thus reducing UK competitiveness and making it difficult for trade deficits and hence interest rates to fall.

Critics of the ERM have suggested that it is little more than a 'deutschmark zone'. Disagreements between member states have made it difficult to envisage progress towards a single currency and central bank as promoted by supporters of the European Monetary System (EMS). While negotiations for a draft treaty were conducted during 1991, some member states put foward rival plans for a 'two-speed Europe' so that countries with a substantially higher rate of inflation than Germany would not immediately join the 'core' of states advancing to monetary union.

Chapter Seven

Impact of membership on the UK

This royal throne of kings, this scept'red isle
This earth of majesty, this seat of Mars,
This other Eden, demi-paradise,

. . . .

With inky blots, and rotten parchment bonds;
That England, that was wont to conquer others,
Hath made a shameful conquest of itself.

John of Gaunt in *Richard II*

There are still some in the UK who see accession to the Community as giving up **sovereignty** – whether they are right or as out of date as John of Gaunt is a matter of personal opinion. Read the boxed report of a speech by Lord Cockfield to hear the opposite view. It may be indicative that the British government disapproved of his enthusiasm for Europe and replaced him in Brussels with Sir Leon Brittan, who rapidly became enthusiastic himself and was accused of 'going native'.

Political opinion in the UK remains split, although predominantly in favour of the Community. The point is well illustrated by the following comments published in *The Spectator* on 14 July 1990; they were made by Mr Ridley, then Minister for the Environment:

> '*When I look at the institutions to which it is proposed that sovereignty is to be handed over, I'm aghast. Seventeen unelected reject politicians with no accountability to anybody, who are not responsible for raising taxes, just spending money, who are pandered to by a supine parliament which also is not responsible for raising taxes, already behaving with an arrogance I find breathtaking – the idea that one says, 'OK, we'll give this lot our sovereignty', is unacceptable to me. I'm not against giving up sovereignty in principle, but not to this lot. You might just as well give it to Adolf Hitler, frankly.*'

After the publication of these views Mr Ridley was quickly forced to resign! Nevertheless many commentators *claimed* that Mr Ridley had only said in public what numerous politicians, including perhaps

THE WEEK IN EUROPE

Lord Cockfield: Income rise to follow 1992. Commission Vice-President, Lord Cockfield, delivered a vigorous defence of the plans for frontier-free Europe by 1992 in a speech before the Swiss Institute for International Studies in Zurich on October 3. He quoted the Cecchini report, predicting a big increase in national income in the Community, a reduction of prices and the creation of millions of new jobs, in support of his argument in favour of the single European economy. Lord Cockfield said he was neither a visionary nor wholly a pragmatist over the future of European union, but believed the Community faced not a crisis but a situation where it was being pulled in different directions all at once. 'The broader issues', he added, 'cannot indefinitely be postponed.' Turning to economic integration, Lord Cockfield said 'the opposition to the Single European currency arises mainly from a fear of a loss of national sovereignty', but added he believed the whole argument to be largely misconceived. 'The Community is based not on a loss of sovereignty but on a pooling of sovereignty; on its exercise jointly in the common good rather than its exercise separately – often selfishly and to the detriment of other people'.

Source: Press Release, Commission of the European Communities, 6 October 1988

the then Prime Minister Mrs Thatcher, believed in private. In November 1990 the deputy Prime Minister, Sir Geoffrey Howe, resigned his post on the grounds that he disagreed profoundly with Mrs Thatcher's approach to the Community. This encouraged Mr Heseltine, who had himself resigned from the Cabinet over a European issue some years previously, to challenge Mrs Thatcher for the Conservative party leadership. The subsequent election competition forced Mrs Thatcher to resign, and Mr John Major became the new Prime Minister. These exciting political events underline the current importance attached to the relationship between the UK and the EC and the depth of controversy which this matter generates. What attitude the UK government now takes under Mr Major remains to be seen, but it is expected to be more 'European'. It is essential for economists to recognize and take account of the political aspects of their analyses, but to remain as far as possible unbiased. So we now turn from noting political events to ask the factual question – what then is the *economic* impact of EC membership?

It is evident that joining the Community has greatly reduced the policy choices available to the British government. More and more decisions are taken by the Community jointly rather than by Britain individually. Thus if the UK has a balance of payments problem, membership rules out the use of import controls, or subsidies to help UK firms. Competition policy is increasingly determined in Brussels. For some years all major policy decisions affecting agriculture and fishing have been taken at Community level. The Single European Market to be completed by the end of 1992 is being achieved through collective decision-making.

As noted in earlier chapters the UK government has not been happy at the prospect of more decisions being transferred to Brussels. The debate over economic and monetary union is the best example of these concerns.

75

The economic benefits of membership

Table 11 gives some of the main economic indicators for the UK economy. It shows that the rate of economic growth was much higher in the decade before accession than in the years immediately following. However, this does not necessarily demonstrate a negative impact of EC membership, the slower growth of the 1970s being easily explained by external events. In 1974 the world price of oil increased by almost 400 per cent, followed by further significant increases at the end of the decade. This was a major factor in precipitating a worldwide depression, so low growth rates were then the norm in all industrialized countries. In the 1980s the UK's economic growth resumed, to an average of about 2.8 per cent, less than the average in the 1960s.

Table 11 Evolution of the UK economy, 1961–90

	1961 to 1973	1974 to 1981	1982	1983	1984	1985	1986	1987	1988	1989	1990*
GDP annual real growth rate(%)	3.2	0.7	1.2	3.8	1.8	3.6	3.1	3.8	4.2	2.2	2.1
Gross fixed capital formation (% share of GDP)	18.5	18.8	16.7	16.1	17.1	17.1	16.9	17.3	18.8	18.8	18.6
Inflation rate	4.8	15.1	8.8	4.8	5.1	5.3	4.4	3.9	5.0	6.1	7.0
Productivity change (%)†	2.9	1.1	3.1	5.1	-0.1	2.0	2.7	1.9	1.0	0.4	1.3
Real unit labour costs index	100	103.0	98.7	97.0	97.6	96.7	97.6	97.7	97.4	98.5	100.3
Employment annual change (%)	0.3	-0.4	-1.8	-1.2	1.9	1.6	0.4	1.9	3.1	1.7	0.7
Unemployment rate (%)	2.0	5.0	10.5	11.2	11.4	11.5	11.5	10.6	8.7	6.8	6.5

* Forecast. † GDP at constant market prices per person employed.

Source: *European Economy,* vol. 42, 1989; and vol. 46, 1990

The UK economy should not be examined in isolation, so how does it compare with the Community average? Table 12 shows that in 1960 the UK enjoyed substantially higher incomes than did the other Community members. By the time of accession the UK had lost this advantage. However, the relative decline seems to have been arrested and the UK is now managing to maintain her relative position. These data must be interpreted with care. They do not prove that membership of the Community has been a good thing, though they are consistent with such a belief, and of course they cannot counter the assertion that the UK would have done even better outside the Community.

Table 12 GDP per head in UK as percentage of EC(12)

1960	127.6
1965	117.8
1970	107.1
1975	105.5
1980	101.1
1985	103.7
1990*	103.7

GDPs are compared in terms of purchasing power standard.
* Forecast.

Source: *European Economy,* vol. 42, 1989

Chapter 2 discussed the theoretical background to economic integration. It concluded that the major economic benefit was the gain from trade resulting from the exploitation of **comparative advantage, specialization** and associated **economies of size.** How has UK trade with the EC progressed since accession? In terms of goods, visible trade, about one-third of UK imports and exports were traded with the EC immediately before accession; this share had gradually increased to be just over a half by 1988. Table 13 shows that the balance of trade has been markedly in favour of the EC during most of the period of UK membership, and the UK's trade balance has been deteriorating rapidly in the latter half of the 1980s. Why has the UK's competitive position worsened in this way? One possible reason is the output of North Sea oil, which increased very quickly at the end of the 1970s to reach a peak in 1985. In only a few years the UK turned from being a major oil importer to being more than self-sufficient. This caused a swift rise in the sterling exchange rate, making British exports relatively expensive, and imports correspondingly cheap. A second explanation is similar in its effect – that government reliance on high interest rates to control inflation forced up the exchange rate, particularly at the end of the 1980s. The UK's poor competitive position resulted in a decline in manufacturing industry. Under such circumstances it is not surprising that the UK balance of trade with the EC has been so one-sided. It must be noted that even in trade in invisibles, where the UK is supposed to have a comparative advantage, the deficit has been growing. However, invisibles have been subject to many restrictions which have tended to prevent the exploitation of comparative advantage.

Table 13 UK trade balance with the EC, 1973–88 (£ million)

	Visible trade	Invisibles	Totals
1973	-1 327	96	-1 231
1974	-2 134	202	-1 932
1975	-2 487	-258	-2 246
1976	-2 186	-195	-3 082
1977	-1 795	-451	-3 228
1978	-2 487	-661	-3 148
1979	-2 683	-481	-3 163
1980	758	-620	138
1981	39	891	930
1982	-1 323	974	-349
1983	-2 675	1 473	-1 202
1984	-3 382	843	-2 539
1985	-2 450	-707	-3 157
1986	-8 761	-509	-9 270
1987	-9 421	-3 380	-12 801
1988	-13 453	-2 886	-16 339

Before 1976, data exclude Spain and Portugal; all current EC members are included in all other years.

Source: CSO 'Pink Books', various years

It is impossible for the UK to reap all the potential benefits of a larger market when her competitive situation is constantly eroded by a rate of inflation which exceeds that of the other main members of the Community, as well as an exchange rate which is artificially high. Tables 9 and 11 show that the rate of inflation in the UK is persistently higher than in most other member countries. A major factor is labour costs – Table 10 shows that these have risen more rapidly in the UK than in major EC competitors. It could be argued that by not joining the ERM of the EMS until now the UK has avoided the benefit of reduced inflation. On the other hand the increased competition of the Single European Market should help to reduce relative labour costs and inflation, but this is a future potential gain rather than a current impact and so must remain to be judged by events. To date, membership of the EC seems to have had little effect on the UK rate of inflation. Indeed, it has probably had even less effect than the UK government's fight against inflation which has proved extremely disappointing after more than a decade of effort.

The problem of agriculture

The Common Agricultural Policy has received more media exposure and criticism in the UK than all the other Community concerns put together. It has indeed had four major negative influences on the UK which will now be discussed.

Misallocation of resources

Because agriculture is heavily protected compared with the relatively minor protection afforded to the manufacturing sector, significant resource misallocation occurs. Within the Community, resources are used by agriculture which could be used more productively in other sectors. High food prices help to push up labour costs and reduce international competitiveness. This is compounded by the dumping of surpluses on world markets, helping to reduce the costs of some competitors (Japan is a major food importer), and making other food exporters poorer with a consequent reduction in their demand for UK or other EC exports.

Trade diversion

Trade diversion is of considerable importance. Before accession the UK purchased food imports at low world market prices. Since accession, much food has been purchased from other Community countries at the high internal prices.

Support costs

The budgetary costs of supporting Community agriculture have fallen disproportionately heavily upon the UK. As noted earlier, expenditure on the CAP dominates the Community's budget. The UK has to contribute its share to supporting this expenditure. As this expenditure is largely for the disposal of agricultural surpluses the recipient countries are those producing these surpluses, which does not include the UK to any great extent. Table 14 illustrates the problem, showing that UK payments to the budget have greatly exceeded receipts. The other Community members admitted that the UK was unfairly treated by the budget mechanism, and from 1980 onwards some refunds were negotiated on an annual *ad hoc* basis. From 1985 these were replaced by reductions in the VAT element of contributions to the budget according to a formula: the rebate to be 66 per cent of the difference between the UK's share of VAT contributions and its share of expenditure. Since the addition of a GNP-related resource to the budget's income in 1988, this is included in the rebate formula. However, these refunds and abatements have still left the UK as a major net contributor to the budget. Between 1973 and 1988 the cumlative net contribution exceeds £10 billion at current market prices; in constant 1990 prices it would be very much more. UK government estimates put the current net contributions at very nearly £2 billion per year. These net contributions, and usually heated negotiations to get them reduced, have frequently soured relations between the UK and other members of the Community.

Table 14 UK transactions with the Community budget (£ million)

	1973	1974	1975	1976	1977	1978	1979	1980	1981	1982	1983	1984	1985	1986	1987	1988
Credits																
Agricultural Fund	63	112	342	207	181	329	371	550	683	791	1082	1353	1203	1385	1344	1379
Social Fund	–	16	19	11	48	63	87	95	107	152	128	283	256	335	428	277
Regional Fund	–	–	–	29	60	35	71	173	145	111	139	184	274	298	404	370
Budget refunds	–	–	–	–	–	–	–	98	693	1019	807	528	61	–	–	–
Other	17	25	38	52	88	107	136	154	152	234	227	230	233	277	222	179
Totals	80	153	400	299	376	533	666	1070	1780	2307	2383	2578	2027	2295	2398	2205
Debits																
Agricultural and sugar levies	9	14	32	38	154	242	247	260	218	307	232	260	189	244	354	226
Customs duties	142	192	320	438	613	714	868	861	861	1001	1075	1276	1291	1244	1417	1521
VAT gross	–	–	–	–	–	596	844	741	1095	1554	1669	1665	2090	3005	3431	2759
VAT abatements*	–	-33	-11	-13	-30	-204	-352	-95	–	–	–	–	-166	-1701	-1153	-1595
Special agreements	–	–	–	–	–	–	–	–	–	–	–	–	370	–	–	613
Other	36	13	9	11	13	16	20	16	14	16	18	12	30	20	17	31
Totals	187	186	350	474	750	1364	1626	1783	2184	2878	2994	3213	3804	2812	4066	3556
Balance	-107	-33	50	-175	-374	-831	-960	-713	-404	-571	-611	-635	-1777	-617	-1668	-1351

* In 1974–80 these were budget adjustments.
Source: CSO 'Pink Books', various years

Environmental costs

Environmental costs of the CAP are also considerable. High cereal prices have persuaded farmers to plough much of the chalk downs, which at world prices would have remained in their traditional use as grazing. So grasslands rich in wildlife – flowers, butterflies, and birds etc. – have been turned into less scenic cornfields whose production adds to cereal surpluses which are expensive to dispose of. This is but one illustration of an extensive catalogue of unnecessary environmental degradation caused by the CAP's high prices.

How much the CAP has cost and is costing the UK is unknown. The four costs identified above fall into three different categories. The simplest is that of exactly known costs which applies to the budgetary transfers. More difficult are the costs of trade diversion and the costs of resource misallocation. These are costs which could only be approximately estimated in relation to various assumptions. A further degree of difficulty is associated with the estimation of environmental costs. For example, how can you value wild flowers, butterflies or a beautiful view? There are methods but at best they must be described as extremely dubious. So politicians tend to ignore all but the budgetary costs of the CAP, and their decisions are related only to these.

Other environmental benefits

Valuing environmental 'goods' and 'bads' may be towards the impossible side of difficult, but they are nevertheless very important to our standard of living. On many of these issues common action is essential because action by individual nations is unlikely. Acid rain is a good example. It is produced largely by burning coal in power stations to produce electricity. Coal is a very variable natural product but always contains some sulphur. So when burnt, sulphurous gases enter the atmosphere resulting in rain which is very dilute sulphuric acid. Acid rain corrodes public buildings (especially those built of limestone), acidifies lakes causing the death of fish, and is thought to be doing great harm in large areas of pine forest throughout northern Europe and particularly in Scandinavia. Removing the sulphurous gases from power station smoke is possible but expensive, and would therefore increase the costs of generating electricity. Consequently a government will be reluctant to increase its costs by desulphurization of power station emissions unilaterally. That the UK is currently preparing to build its first power station desulphurization plants is due to Community pressure, not UK government enthusiasm.

Community action is also apparent in respect of water pollution. In recent years much has been heard of the need for the UK to clean up its drinking water supplies and its beaches. Unlike the air pollution discussed above, curing these forms of pollution would not have a significant impact on industrial costs. Yet the pace of developments here again owes more to Community legislation than to UK government actions.

Is membership of the Community a good thing?

At the time of writing the UK has been a member of the Community for 17 years. Has membership been of net economic benefit so far and what of the future? Looking at the past, a conclusion is surprisingly difficult. The most widely known consequence of membership is the high budgetary costs to the UK of the CAP. Other costs and benefits are difficult to estimate. One pointer is that prior to membership the UK's GDP was growing more slowly than the average for the Community, but has more recently kept pace (Table 12). Unfortunately this information is capable of very different interpretations; it might be argued, for example, that outside the Community the UK's relative economic decline could have been reversed more effectively. No definitive answer to these questions is possible.

It is, perhaps, too soon to attempt to assess whether membership of the Community is economically beneficial to the UK. The single market stage with its expected substantial benefits is only now in the process of being achieved. If the economic analysis of Chapter 2 is valid, then the UK, together with all other members, will benefit in the long run.

KEY WORDS

Sovereignty	Specialization
Comparative advantage	Economies of size

Reading list

National Institute of Economic and Social Research, *The UK Economy*, Heinemann Educational, 1990 (particularly Chapters 6 and 7).

Venables, T., 'The international competitiveness of the UK economy', *Economic Review*, March 1990.

Essay topic

How has Britain's membership of the EEC benefited Britain and the European Community as a whole?

Data Response Question 6

This task is based on a WJEC examination question in 1987. Study the statistics in the table, which is taken from the *National Institute Economic Review* of November 1984. Then answer the questions.

1. Briefly describe the similarities and differences between the two economies as shown in the table.
2. What is indicated regarding relative standards of living? What qualifications would you deem it necessary to make in drawing conclusions from the figures?

3. What broad factors might account for the higher level of output per worker in France?
4. Despite similar levels of government expenditure as a proportion of GDP the percentage employed in General Government in France is lower. What might account for this?
5. In both countries gross fixed capital formation considerably exceeds net household savings. What additional sources of funds may finance the higher level of capital formation?

The French and British economies compared (1981)

	France	UK
Population (mid-year)	53,963,000	56,020,000
GDP (US $ billion)	538.7	467.5
GDP per capita (US $)	9,982	8,346
Gross fixed capital formation (% of GDP)	21.2	15.9
Net household savings ratio (% of disposable income)	12.2	8.7
Total civilian employment	20,959,000	23,819,000
Labour force (as per cent of population)	43.0	47.7
Percentage employed in		
Industry	35.3	35.9
Agriculture	8.5	2.6
General Government	15.8	22.0
Total outlays of government (% of GDP)	49.2	48.0
Exports (goods and services as % of GDP)	23.8	27.4
Imports (goods and services as % of GDP)	25.3	24.5
Output per employed worker-year (1980) (thousand 1973 $)	14.2	9.2
Output per employed worker-year in manufacturing	12.8	6.8
Output per employed worker-year in agriculture	8.1	10.7

Data Response Question 7

This task is based on a University of London School Examinations Board question in 1989. The data in the table and the three figures (taken from *The Economist* of 24 January 1987) present some comparative statistics on the performance of two economies, Great

Britain and Italy. Study the data and then answer the following questions.

1. What does Figure A indicate about the changes in the standard of living in Britain and Italy in the period 1955–1987?
2. Comment on the relationship between inflation and unemployment in the two countries as shown in Figures B and C.
3. Suggest reasons which might explain this relationship in each country.
4. How might you account for the different trends in the share of world exports of manufactured goods accounted for by Britain and Italy?

GDPs for period 1955–1987

	Great Britain	Italy
	(figures in £ billions)	
1955	19	9
1965	36	22
1975	106	86
1987	396	408

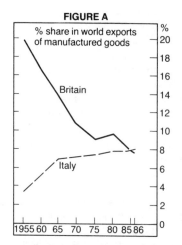

FIGURE A

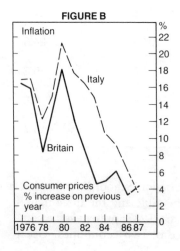

FIGURE B

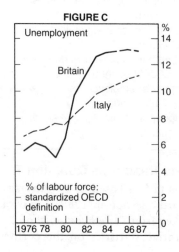

FIGURE C

Chapter Eight

Progress and prospects

All for one and one for all – Dumas

When one now observes the progress of economic and political integration in the Community, it is difficult to believe that it is only 45 years since the end of the Second World War. That war involved the four largest EC members as some of the main antagonists, two on one side, two on the other. It was separated from a similar preceding war by only one generation. If the coming together in the Community of these previously warring factions had no other effect than to prevent a further war, the Community would be a great economic success, for even ignoring the human costs, the economic waste of those two wars was enormous. The prevention of war seems a rather negative benefit; this chapter now looks at the positive side, the economic progress which has been achieved and the prospects for further progress in a Europe of rapid and accelerating change.

The economic success of the Community

During the past thirty years the economies of the twelve have grown more rapidly than that of the USA. As Table 15 shows, in 1960 the

Table 15 GDP per head: EC compared with USA and Japan, 1960–90

	EC(12) = 100	
	USA	*Japan*
1960	189	56
1965	182	68
1970	164	91
1975	155	94
1980	152	101
1985	157	112
1990 (forecast)	152	117

The comparison is in terms of purchasing power standard.
Source: *European Economy*, vol. 42, 1989

GDP per head in the USA was 89 per cent higher than that in the Community, and by 1990 the American lead was a little over 50 per cent. Over the same period Japanese GDP per head has rocketed from being 55 per cent of that in the Community to gaining a lead of 17 per cent. The report on Community progress must be 'satisfactory but could do better!'

Table 16 EC economic recovery in the 1980s

	1960–73	1973–81	1981–84	1984–87	1987–90*
Growth of GDP (real annual)	4.8	1.9	1.6	2.6	3.4
Employment change (annual %)	0.3	-0.1	-0.5	0.8	1.4
Inflation rate	4.6	12.3	8.7	4.4	4.3
Balance on current account (as % GDP)	0.4	-0.3	-0.1	1.0	0.2
	1973	1981	1984	1987	1990*
Unemployment (%)	2.8	8.1	10.8	10.4	8.7
Capacity utilization (%)	85.8	77.4	79.0	83.0	86.0

* Forecast.

Source: *European Economy*, vol. 42, 1989

Economic growth has been very variable during the Community's first three decades. Table 16 shows that initially growth was rapid, but worldwide recessions, largely caused by oil price shocks in 1974 and again in 1979, greatly reduced growth, and led to the underemployment of resources in general and labour in particular. After 1984 growth began to accelerate but unemployment, although falling, remained high compared with the 1960s. The Commission attributes the improvements in the 1980s to two main factors: the Community's success in reducing inflation, and the implementation of **supply-side policies** from the beginning of the decade. The latter have encouraged a marked increase in investment in equipment and the growth of capital productivity. It is claimed that the prospect of the single European market is helping to sustain further investment and growth.

Completion of the internal market

The Community White Paper of June 1985, which led to the Single European Act, listed 279 actions necessary for the completion of the internal market. By the end of 1989 the

Commission had tabled all of these and well over half had been passed by the Council. The qualified majority voting system used since the SEA has, as intended, greatly speeded the rate at which Council decisions are taken. There is no doubt that the flow of directives and regulations will see most of the required legislation passed before the end of the 1992 deadline.

Much publicity has been given to the approaching Single European Market in an attempt to prepare businesses for the increased levels of competition. In the UK the Department of Trade and Industry has produced booklets, pamphlets and two videos, and also operates an extensive telephone helpline system. Chambers of Commerce, trade associations and other organizations have been organizing conferences and seminars all over the country since 1987.

Firms throughout the Community are responding to the larger market in a variety of ways. Many industrial firms are planning increased capacity to cope with extra demand, distribution networks are being expanded and products changed to suit different markets. When multinationals have production units in several member states some are being closed so that potential economies of size can be exploited in the remainder. In both industry and services there has been a surge in the number of takeovers and mergers, particularly across national boundaries.

Economic and political union

Economic and monetary union seems to be progressing steadily despite opposition by the UK government. With the rapidity of change seen in eastern Europe during 1990 even wider unions are being planned. Most obvious is the addition of East Germany to the Community in October 1990. This has proceeded not as the accession of a new country, but via unification with West Germany. Upon unification the main body of Community law had immediate effect in the former East Germany. For example, 80 per cent of directives laying down technical rules applied at once. The Commission is requesting flexibility in making transitional arrangements so that special aid measures can be taken to restructure the East German economy. The CAP should apply by 1992, but to reduce inflationary pressure food subsidies will be phased out slowly over several years.

Applications for Community membership have been received from Austria, Turkey, Cyprus and Malta (in that order). The governments of Czechoslovakia and Sweden have announced their intentions to apply. Other European countries, particularly in the east, seem likely to follow. Against this background the Commission has produced a plan for a wider economic and political union in western Europe which might eventually be extended to include some east European countries. The Commission's plan is for what it calls 'European Economic Space', comprising EC and EFTA and Liechtenstein. The objective would be to incorporate the EFTA members' (Austria, Finland, Iceland, Norway and Sweden) economies as closely as possible into the European single market. EFTA members would have to apply EC rules on trade and competition, and at the political level would in future be consulted when the Community was making decisions affecting these issues. The essence of the proposal is to form a wide **customs union** within which goods, services and capital would be free to move, but labour would not. Free movement of labour, if the EC was extended to include eastern Europe, could result in mass uncontrolled 'economic migration'. The plan seems a sensible, cautious approach to further economic integration.

Current problems

There are two pressing economic problems for the Community. The first relates to the large differences in GNP per head between member states. In the two poorest states, Greece and Portugal, GNP per head is only half that in the richer members, indeed only a little over half of the Community average. Ireland and Spain, respectively at three-quarters and two-thirds of the average, are also notable. Differences between the other eight members are relatively small, and all are above the average. So much more real economic convergence, by raising average GNP in the poorer states, is required. The Community is assisting to this end, most notably by improving the **infrastructures** of the poorer regions and countries.

The second economic problem concerns trade, particularly in agricultural products. As the world's largest trading bloc the community can significantly influence the state of world trade. When the Single European Act was passed many countries feared that the single market would encourage the Community to become inward-looking and protectionist – 'fortress Europe'. These fears are proving to be unfounded, but further liberalization of world trade depends on the outcome of the Uruguay round of trade negotiations in GATT. In turn this depends to a considerable extent on the willingness of the Community to reduce the levels of protection which it affords to agriculture.

On the political front the political weakness of the Community has been exposed by the Gulf crisis. As individual states the

Community members have condemned the Iraqi invasion of Kuwait. Some have sent forces to the Gulf, but they represent individual members, not the Community as a whole. This crisis has shown that the current political cooperation and foreign policy coordination of the Community results in a slow and fragmented response to emergencies. The Commission will doubtless continue to work for ever closer **political union**.

Retrospect and prospect

Over the years the Community has grown from its original six members to nine, to ten, to twelve, and still more countries wish to join. Clearly in the eyes of many the Community has been a success and this is expected to continue. The single market promises to enhance the Community's development – already it is the world's largest market in terms of population. As Adam Smith observed, 'specialization is limited by the extent of the market' – meaning that efficiency depends on market size. With current developments the Community has the potential to become, within a generation, the world's major economic power.

KEY WORDS

Supply-side policies	Infrastructures
Customs union	Political union

Further reading

Readers may keep up to date with Community developments by reading any of the 'quality' newspapers. Coverage is particularly good in *The Economist*, *The Times*, the *Financial Times*, and the *Independent*.

Essay topics

1. Discuss the economic organization of the Community in terms of the gains from economic integration which were analysed in Chapter 2.
2. Explain carefully why the evidence in Table 16 does or does not convince you that the Community economy improved during the 1980s.

Index